Whiteness and Antiracism

Whiteness and Antiracism

Beyond White Privilege Pedagogy

Kevin Lally

Foreword by Samuel Jaye Tanner

TEACHERS COLLEGE PRESS

TEACHERS COLLEGE | COLUMBIA UNIVERSITY
NEW YORK AND LONDON

Published by Teachers College Press,® 1234 Amsterdam Avenue, New York, NY 10027

Copyright © 2022 by Teachers College, Columbia University

Front cover image by Ivan Bastien / iStock by Getty Images.

Library of Congress Cataloging-in-Publication Data is available at loc.gov

ISBN 978-0-8077-6662-0 (paper)
ISBN 978-0-8077-6663-7 (hardcover)
ISBN 978-0-8077-8086-2 (ebook)

Printed on acid-free paper
Manufactured in the United States of America

For my children, Jack and Greta

If whiteness gains currency by being unnoticed, then what does it mean to notice whiteness? . . . We could say that any project that aims to dismantle or challenge the categories that are made invisible through privilege is bound to participate in the object of its critique. We might even expect such projects to fail, and be prepared to witness this failure as productive.

—Sara Ahmed

Contents

Foreword

There should be more books like this.

That's the first thing I want to tell you. I'll tell you two other things, but I want to start by writing that I wish more people wrote about teaching and learning like Kevin Lally does here.

There's an intimacy in this book, an honesty often missing in writing about education. I've never met Kevin in person, yet I left this book feeling as though I had. At moments I felt like one of his students, at other times a colleague, a teacher down the hall, or a scholar across the table, thinking hard with Kevin. I am another White person who is serious about following Tim Lensmire's (2008) lead to "become smarter" about my Whiteness, and Kevin's book invited me into that important work and helped me get smarter.

Kevin doesn't offer a well-ordered recipe for how White people should confront and make sense of Whiteness here. I've learned to be leery of such books. Instead, Kevin tells a unique story about something he tried to do. And in so telling this story (and telling it well), he makes room for others to try and do something else. To live and teach differently. To, as Kevin puts it, get unstuck.

And that's the second thing I want to tell you about this book. I hope reading it unsticks you.

As I read this book, I thought about Billy Pilgrim, Kurt Vonnegut's protagonist in *Slaughterhouse-Five* who gets unstuck in time. Billy came to mind when Kevin wrote about how most of his experience with antiracist pedagogy had left him feeling stuck. Particularly White privilege pedagogy. Kevin's argument reminded me that good pedagogy moves us beyond scripts. It leaves us unstuck in space and time. *Slaughterhouse-Five* came to mind again as Kevin's student Ben described what his participation in discussions of Whiteness had accomplished. Ben used the metaphor of pigs hanging in a slaughterhouse with their insides spilling out. Gruesome, right?

Talk about a summative assessment.

I'm so thankful for the teachers who have helped me to open myself up and look squarely at my life, at who I am and how I move through the world. Ben's comment, to me, honors the transformative possibility of Kevin's teaching. It also affirms the notion of critical Whiteness pedagogy Kevin is writing toward—an approach that is messy, a little gruesome, and urgently needed if White people are going to do battle with White supremacy. Kevin's work to make the history of White supremacy and contemporary evocations of Whiteness visible to White people is timely to say the least.

It's the winter of 2022 as I write this foreword. White supremacy flourishes in the United States. My ongoing work to wrestle with Whiteness leaves me convinced that trying to do and say the right thing isn't going to liberate White people, myself included, from participating in the evil of White supremacy. It's an evil that leads to death and destruction for people of color and, according to writer Toni Morrison during a 1998 interview with Charlie Rose, causes White people in the United States to suffer from a "profound neurosis" that has a "deleterious effect" on them. White people need to live differently, and we need teachers to show us how. We need to come unstuck so that we might become something new. Something healthier. I think Kevin's book helps, so I hope you'll get unstuck as you read it.

Here's the third thing I want to write about Kevin's book. Being a good teacher is hard. Writing honestly about good teaching is even harder. Kevin, so far as I see it, has accomplished both things. I'm always moved when I encounter the kind of teaching and writing that you'll find in this book.

So consider this an invitation into something important. I hope you'll stick it out and, in so doing, come unstuck. Here's a spoiler alert: Kevin Lally ends this book by wondering if we, especially White people, can have a heightened awareness of the ways in which all of us are connected. After reading this book, I felt more connected with Kevin, his students, and his stories. I hope you'll leave this book feeling the same way. Changed a little bit. And in so being changed, I hope you'll create and share your own stories of trying to live differently.

God knows we need those kinds of stories right now.

—*Samuel Jaye Tanner*

REFERENCES

Lensmire, T. J. (2008). How I became White while punching de tar baby. *Curriculum Inquiry, 38*(3), 299–322. http://www.jstor.org/stable/25475908

Morrison, T. (1998, January 19). *An hour with Nobel prize winner Toni Morrison* [Interview by C. Rose]. https://charlierose.com/videos/31212

Acknowledgments

To the young White people who generously offered your time, wisdom, and vulnerability in my "experiment" about Whiteness, I am humbled by your trust in me and this project. Thank you.

To my friends and colleagues at St Ann's: you have shared, listened, struggled, and celebrated with me as we endeavored to do right by the young people in our classrooms. Your camaraderie and solidarity sustained me through this process. Thank you.

To my parents: You raised me to look out for others and to think for myself. For your foundation of critical thinking and compassion, thank you.

To my friend and mentor, Tim: your kindness, insight, and humor set me on this path of working to make sense of Whiteness a decade ago, and then got me in this predicament of turning it all into a book. Thank you. (Seriously, thank you.)

To my friends and collaborators, especially Ben and Ellie: your friendship keeps me laughing, embodied, and attentive to what matters. For your encouragement, accountability, and love, thank you.

To my spouse, my love, Corinne: for your constant reminder of the inherent goodness in all of us, and for your relentless support of me and my work, thank you.

CHAPTER 1

Feeling Stuck

If you don't understand yourself, you don't understand anybody else.

—Nikki Giovanni

I've felt guilty, in one form or another, for some reason or another, for most of my life. I was raised Irish Catholic. Guilt and shame are more familiar to me than the happiness that comes from feeling uncomplicatedly connected to the people around me. I'm familiar with guilt; I know what it feels like. Guilt is a thing inside my belly, a heaviness. Shame, too, has made itself at home in my body, and while it is deeper and broader and more caustic than the weightiness of guilt, it also is a burden with which I am familiar.

My Whiteness[1] is neither an acid nor a weight. While I contend with my Whiteness daily, and find it between me and my whole self, it does not feel burdensome. In fact, before I learned the histories of race and Whiteness in the United States, my Whiteness registered to me as an absence, an emptiness.

The guilt I was encouraged to feel for the horrors of White supremacy registered differently in me than my own guilt and shame; I felt them not as sins of my forefathers but as the suffering of people I was made to think of as different than me. In short, Whiteness never felt like it was about *me*. Even my own Whiteness felt remote, an aspect of my identity that barely registered as I moved through my primarily White world.

As a young person, I was introduced to my Whiteness through the lens of White privilege, wherein my well-intentioned White teachers encouraged us, their White students, to recognize our Whiteness as a kind of academic problem. We were to make sense of it, to tackle it in our brains through conversation and reflection, which were then assessed for understanding and comprehension. However, if we were to make different decisions or understand the world in different ways, that was never clarified for us. Moreover, we were never encouraged to *be* different. Like the rest of my education, my body had nothing to do with it.

The ways I was told to become aware of my Whiteness, while sensible, were intangible. Whatever privilege I accrued by nature of being White were either challenging for me to recognize or beyond my capacity to remedy. I could not, for example, change how people saw me, nor could I avoid looking like those in positions of power. I believed I had privileges because of my skin color, though many of the financial privileges listed in McIntosh's (1988) "Invisible Knapsack" felt abstract to me, and others, like finding flesh-colored bandages that matched my skin tone, seemed trite in the context of the seriousness of racism. I also struggled to conceptualize and appreciate the ways I was *not* encumbered by racial discrimination, such as not being followed in a store or not being called upon to represent my race. Despite *knowing* the importance of White privilege, and believing that I had it, I struggled to convert that knowledge into something that felt meaningful.

Relatedly, and perhaps most importantly, I was entirely unaware of the profound mechanisms of Whiteness within my psyche, the very real way Whiteness distanced me both psychically and physically from others. I only knew my discomfort, blunt and disembodied, when I encountered the boundaries of Whiteness. I could never have named it at the time, but I could feel what Thandeka (2001) calls the non-White zones around and within me: geographic, ideological, musical, and ways of being. The 24-hour Perkins in the working-class and racially mixed neighborhood where I grew up was "ghetto" to my wealthier White classmates. At home, I could critique racism but not without also paying homage to individual effort, and "Black" music was good so long as it predated the early 1990s. However, I could never sag my pants or swagger, at home or at school. Whiteness dictated each of these boundaries. As real, as enforced, and as meaningful as these boundaries were, they were never talked about as being White, if they were talked about at all.

This unmentioned Whiteness, ethereal, insidious, and dangerous, underscored our classroom conversations about White privilege. The discomfort of the bounds of Whiteness was never addressed by my White teachers; indeed, if there is an opposite of addressing discomfort, that's what happened. Ironically, while our White teachers might tell us that it would be hard or even uncomfortable to examine our White privileges, the actual discomfort we all experienced when the topic of race came up was studiously avoided. Instead, we all stuck to the script of White privilege and hoped that the unit would pass without incident. Importantly, given the tense or anxious tones in which Whiteness was addressed by my teachers, I was to contend with my Whiteness as an individual, which reinforced my guilt and shame. I was on my own.

This is not to say that the work was not challenging, that no one changed, or that nothing was gained. Yet the stilted sincerity of White privilege antiracist work limited my classroom pedagogy in profound and unseen ways.

* * *

I began teaching fresh out of college. I was 23 and idealistic, and I was hired to teach English in the high school from which I had graduated, affording me a false sense of competence. I brought with me my own expensive education, full of well-meaning and earnest teachers who worked to open my eyes to the world using the best tools available. My students were almost entirely White and financially secure like me in this private Catholic school. I embodied that dangerous combination of confidence and good intentions.

As a White high school teacher, I understood the racial views I was to address as a kind of innocent misunderstanding. I believed that there were really only two ways to interpret racial inequality: either structural racisms cause racial inequality, or races are inherently unequal. Clearly my good White high school students would not want to make that second claim, so my work on race should be relatively straightforward. I was to introduce them to and convince them of racial inequalities so that they would recognize the structural racisms that I had recognized. That was it, that was the work. It was simple, if not always easy.

One of the first units I developed when I began teaching English to 11th graders paired Richard Wright's (2005) *Native Son* and the first chapter of Paolo Freire's (2007) *Pedagogy of the Oppressed*. My pedagogical goal was to contextualize Bigger Thomas's actions within 1930s Chicago's oppressive racist structure using Freire's vocabulary and concepts from *Pedagogy of the Oppressed*. I intended to foreclose the argument that racism is over. I believed if I could demonstrate the existence of structural racism, handily identifiable using Freire, my students would be convinced. In a way, I believed I had solved the problem of teaching White kids about racism; I just had to prove the systemic nature of racism. I was proud of this unit, and I believe it helped a lot of students recognize how systemic oppression operated. It also fell short in worrying ways.

My classroom looked the way I believed it was supposed to look. My students were quiet, watchful, and circumspect in what they shared out loud, which I read as respect for and engagement with the subject matter. These were honors students, which meant they typically acted like they enjoyed English class, were compliant, and were primarily White. Honors students at St Ann's tended to be the kind of students who did their reading and handed their assignments in on time. They also tended to dutifully follow directions and desired to get the answers right. By conventional standards they were very easy to teach.

Yet our conversations about race followed a predictable and troubling pattern. A few students, often supported by a few others, would express skepticism about or resist outright my contextual read of *Native Son* and racism in what became familiar ways. Some White students, typically young men, would push back by citing statistical or anecdotal exceptions, questioning the reality of these racist systems, or make nonverbal moves like exchanging knowing looks or side comments. I felt I could sometimes witness my lessons fail their sense of right and wrong, having come up against the rules of fairness, or their personal experiences of social power. The young White people also had a seductive common sense on their side. Their appeals to post-racialism, including the wealth of LeBron James or Oprah, Obama's presidency, or the struggles of working-class White people, had a canny irrefutability to them.

In response, I or another "woke" student, often a young White woman, would counter them with the zeal and sincerity of a convert. Yet our arguments relied on the less visible legacies of historic racism and structural violence against which practiced and commonsense counterarguments were ready to hand. Sometimes these exchanges took on an implicitly personal tone, with the more aggressive comments mostly coming from students arguing that we must acknowledge White privilege. The more progressive White students chastised their White classmates. I recognized that I had sanctioned these comments and knew that they shut down other students, yet I also struggled to censure them. I worried I would embolden the other side or shut down the woke student themself. Everyone, including me, was anxious, on a knife's edge. I expected these kinds of moments, believing they indicated that I was on the right track, that I was doing the work. At times I found the exchanges thrilling, though mostly they felt exhausting.

Often, these exchanges concerned language. A student might offer a question or observation and refer to "colored people." I would interject and try to explain people-first language, how "colored people" is derogatory, and the phrase was not appropriate. I sometimes took pains to name this as an innocent mistake, even if another student responded first, but the damage was always already done. That student became suspected of being racist, a damaging and durable label in almost any context.

I understood my White students during these conversations in one of two ways: they had either already acknowledged the reality of systemic racism or they needed to do so. I had little awareness of White students beyond these terms. Those who needed to acknowledge racism fell along a continuum of resistances, from those who had not been paying attention to those who spent too much time in the darker corners of the internet. By and large these students and I got along well; I prided myself on being asked one year to be the faculty advisor for a young conservatives' club. But during our work with race, I oriented myself across a battlefield from them. My attitude could best be described as evangelism, as distasteful as that is to me. I believed I was doing God's work.

Even if students were quiet, I believed that I could identify their resistance in their physical posture. They would avoid eye contact, doodle in their notebook, or make side comments to other students. I spent a great deal of energy carefully surveilling my students during these conversations, and I tended to over-surveil the young White men. Occasionally I was surprised to read a conservative reflection from a young White woman, and my lack of attention to my own Whiteness meant I was slow to recognize the biases of my criteria.

Nevertheless, in many ways I believed I was winning at antiracist pedagogy. Our conversations mirrored and referenced national political discourses around race, which was exactly what I thought should happen. I was dealing with a difficult topic using a text some would consider impossible for high school students. When I shared this work with colleagues and friends, I was praised for facilitating open dialogue about race.

I felt delighted when the conversation maintained a basic decency, its own kind of success. Moreover, if these conversations were working, and I was making them work, I must be a good teacher. Much more importantly, by doing this work I was a good *White* teacher. I talked about this work with modesty, humble bragging about how challenging it was, or complaining about how few students seemed affected. My colleagues always affirmed me, that I was doing good work. In reality, it made little difference how effective my pedagogy was; so long as I was taking up this good work, I was a good White teacher. This was a long sought-after relief to be sure, and it all but assured that the unit would remain in place as it was.

Yet even when these classroom conversations seemed to edge toward recognizing racism, or rather when the class makeup was such that those arguments prevailed, I felt unsatisfied, as did many students. We appeared to have arrived at a hard-fought goal, yet it did not feel that way. Even outspokenly antiracist students seemed caught; they knew that not being racist was not enough, but they struggled to come up with what came next. In truth, so did I. The overwhelming feeling after almost all of these conversations, those that went well and those that went poorly, was stagnation. We never seemed to *get* anywhere. Eventually the unit ended, and we moved on. Even with all of us doing our level best to tackle racism, we were poorly equipped to do so.

WHAT HAPPENED

In a dynamic familiar to many teachers who do classroom work with race, very few, if any, students "converted." Additionally, very few White students seemed new to the conversations and what Leslie Margolin (2015) called a "White privilege pedagogy" (WPP) model about race. Most came into my room having encountered some kind of antiracist pedagogy, typically McIntosh's (1988) invisible knapsack, and had their opinions of White privilege ready to hand. The students who accepted the antiracist framework of White privilege, those who identified as White allies especially, nodded along to classroom activities detailing racism and were vocal in small and large group conversations. They reinforced my lesson plans and occasionally provided additional stories or information to strengthen the case for the existence of racial inequality. Yet these students typically brought their views with them. Further, even if they fully embraced their privilege, that move in itself did not seem to resonate much in their lives. I was also suspicious of their confession; it almost seemed *easy*. I wondered if they were only trying to say what they were supposed to say, or just trying to alleviate their own White guilt. Our exchanges felt like a rehearsal, like a scripted dialogue we parroted to each other. Over time I felt a nagging doubt that I was rehashing difficult conversations in unhelpful ways.

Moreover, as the goal of the unit was to convert reluctant White students to an antiracist paradigm, the students who resisted played an essential role of object to be acted upon and converted. When they shared arguments or concerns, I listened so that I might recognize and rebut them. And while some students pushed back out loud, most students stayed quiet during these exchanges. As the teacher facilitating these conversations, I was meant to be an impartial referee. Yet I needed students to resist so I could provide my counterarguments and play my role. Without verbal resistance, my role as converter was undermined. This dynamic felt like an open secret. I was not really an impartial facilitator (nor should I be, as I will explore later), open dialogue was a complicated target when charged, and harmful views were always an off-hand comment away. I got the sense that most students simply waited these units out, hoping to avoid saying the wrong thing. And I could not convince myself that they were all resisting.

At best, I engineered my classwork so that students provided these lessons to themselves and each other through collaborative research projects and presentations. At worst, I was asking them to mobilize White guilt to police their peers' dissonant White voices into acknowledging White supremacy. At the time I failed to appreciate the complex and powerful forces behind White student silences and resistances, factors I now believe to be helpful in making sense of a wide range of student views and behavior in conversations about race. Had I not been bewildered by my own placated anxiety about race and my Whiteness, I certainly would have recognized the structural shortcomings of this unit earlier.

I imagine that these dynamics, and likely many of the frustrations, feel familiar, even to those outside of the classroom. My conversations with family and friends follow the same pattern as my classroom. Race comes up, and with it White privilege, and the familiar lines are drawn. Folks exchange anecdotes and research data or debate the details of a recent incidence of police brutality. And whether any concessions are made, the conversations are often so inscribed they rarely move beyond the White people having them. People seem stuck.

My teaching lacked a critical perspective that could redirect my work toward examining dominant ideologies and Whiteness itself. I struggled to escape the binary logic of neoliberalism[2] where one either was or was not a racist as an individual. My pedagogy was not interested in *why* these students resisted. Tellingly, not once during my early years of working to address race did I think to shift our focus away from people of color, away from a privilege model that high-lighted the subjugation of Black, Indigenous, people of color (BIPoC)[3] folks, casting Whiteness as conqueror which must, out of guilt, atone for or return its ill-gotten gains. It took careful study, reflection, and conversation with scholars to recognize potential antiracist pedagogy unbound by neoliberalism.

Ultimately, who I thought I should be as a good White person en-abled and constrained my pedagogy. I believed my role as a White per-son was to convince other White people that racism was, at its heart, a bad deal. I was not always clear on how bad it was, or in what ways it was bad, and I gave suspiciously little thought to what might happen if I actually managed to convince other White people (to say nothing of how to encourage those who had already confessed). To be gentle with myself, I was following the example of my White educators and colleagues, all wise and compassionate teachers. We were all doing the work we knew to do, and while we celebrated each other, we also pushed through resistance from students, parents, and occasionally our coworkers or administrators. Doing any kind of antiracist work, any kind of social justice advocacy, takes courage and tenacity and is worth celebrating. It is only in hindsight that this practice became self-evidently flawed, and it is only from this experience that I was able to develop my antiracist practice.

I believe the unit worked because it worked for me, and it similarly suffered from my limited self-awareness and limited understanding about the mechanisms of Whiteness. I, like almost all of my students, was White, had attended a private, Catholic, and White grade school before this private, Catholic, and White high school. I had lived in White neighborhoods my entire life. The same expensive (and mostly White) college education I received almost certainly lay ahead of them. The methods of WPP were accessible, familiar, and, especially now that I was on the other side of the classroom, tolerable. By pay-ing careful attention to my students as well as by applying my own experience as a White student, I became skilled at my role of facilitat-ing conversations and working to convince resistant students. I rec-ognized these skills by how adeptly I was able to respond to student resistance, by my command of racial histories, statistics, and anec-dotes, and by the affection my students and I (mostly) felt for each other throughout the work.

Yet despite becoming more and more practiced in this pedagogy, I felt like I was becoming more skilled at a failing venture. I felt like

I was in a futile arms race with resistant students, where every argument served as something to counter without any argument ever landing. While I knew that my work in teaching *Native Son* was to locate Bigger Thomas as a native son of his oppressive environment, I became caught up in my role as a facilitator of these conversations and maintained little self-awareness of our work.

During my years of attempting to engage White students about race, I was hindered by many of these dynamics, occasionally of my own doing. I regularly contended with protesting students, who persuasively called upon Western neoliberal notions of individuality and fairness, with the sinking feeling that however wrong I believed their conclusions, I struggled to explain *why*. Beyond that, I sometimes found myself struggling to parse the differences between a conservative embrace of individualism and meritocracy that celebrated colorblindness as an antiracist position, and, on the other hand, a slightly more progressive celebration of color and the confessions of White racism as antiracism, to students too anxious to truly listen.

I want to reiterate that I was practicing WPP as it was taught to me, and as many of my friends and colleagues practiced it. If we recognized its shortcomings, we did so as we recognize the incompleteness of any pedagogy. WPP met an important need within antiracist pedagogy in the late 1980s and has served to reorient conversation away from those who suffer from White supremacy and toward those who profit by it. In the same way language evolves over time in response to social changes, WPP is no longer the most appropriate tool available for antiracism. I encourage myself, as I encourage you, to honor and work beyond WPP in our classroom practice. It remains central to White peoples' experience and understanding of race and race talk, as I explore in Chapter 2, and our antiracist work must address it.

I FELT STUCK

While I comforted and exonerated myself by blaming White supremacy and assuring myself that I was fighting a good fight, this strategy fell short. By entrenching unhelpful models of race and Whiteness, it may have caused harm to my resisting students year after year. Because the White privilege model permits only two positions, students were either antiracist, which they performed in my *Native Son* unit by sympathizing with Bigger, or they were racist. Those skeptical of my antiracism must have quickly recognized that regardless of their reasoning, their position was unacceptable in my classroom. These White students often left the room angry and defensive—and no wonder, they were being attacked! And worse, the attacks intolerably came from either a teacher or other students who believed that they were sanctioned by the goodness of antiracism. Because their vocal resistance, resistance that I sometimes dragged from them to enable my role as converter, caused them to be targeted as racist, an indelible accusation for a White person, most of the students struggling with antiracism, and many who did not, sought refuge in silence.

I was both sympathetic and critical of this position. I would have been one of those silent students in high school, bothered by racism but too afraid to speak out against it. Even vocal students have psychologically checked out for the duration of a unit or conversation on racism. Many students mastered a prisoner's blank, impassive face to deflect both inquisition and discipline. To my righteous battle-ready mind, the antiracist position was a relatively simple one to take, and vocal resistance was honest, if in need of correction. Silence seemed like a coward's way out. Because there was an obvious cost of resisting the antiracist position (accusations of racism), the only explanation available to me, per the model of White privilege, for why so many students chose to take that risk was that they clung to their privilege. I forgot, or ignored, that all people want to be good, and that there must be goodness on offer from a White identity that denied the existence of White privilege.

My White students, and I myself, desire urgently to feel safe, especially while talking about race, in no small part due to these kinds of conversations. Both available positions were fraught: those who resisted risked being shamed as a racist; students who confessed risked alienating themselves from their White peers. Yet both choices available to White students also offered goodness and safety: either the good, guilty, Whiteness of confession and alignment with the antiracist curriculum, or the good, however shameful, alignment with Whiteness. I did not recognize that the resistance of White students likely came from a desire for goodness in the eyes of their White parents and White society. Thandeka (2001) describes how young White people are forced to choose between the human connection of interracial relationships and the comfort and familiarity of their White family and society. The loss of those relationships causes White shame, says Thandeka. The two available identities in my classroom required that they face that decision again. Understandably, some White students were unwilling to make that choice publicly; the risks were too great.

Further, because of the potency of being accused of racism, students were hesitant to volunteer anything that might put them at risk of being accused and simultaneously eager to discover racism elsewhere in the world, including within their peers. The intense social pressure to be not racist encouraged students to point the finger at others to avoid blame themselves. My students and I were all on the watch for anyone who spoke out of turn, either by denying the impact of Bigger's racist society or by blaming Bigger too severely for his antisocial thoughts and actions. This fostered a tense, accusatory atmosphere that occasionally erupted. When a White student named Sheila wrote in an online forum that if Bigger were White, his racism would put him at the head of the KKK, this pressure erupted. A student of color asked that she apologize. She did and was quickly stigmatized as racist. Sheila seemed to become socially isolated and transferred to another school the following year.

By perpetuating the false binary of racist and antiracist put forward by the White privilege model, I had, unwittingly, deployed the social pressure of racial anxiety to police the classroom discourse, and it had gotten away from me. While our discussions about race often felt like successes (or forgivable failures) to me, the opposing threats of White guilt and White shame had made honest classroom conversation about race all but impossible, and posed real risks to my students. There was safety in silence.

OVERVIEW

This text works through my process of getting smarter about Whiteness. Whiteness is a part of who White people are; it informs our values and ways of being so that challenging Whiteness can feel like challenging our innermost selves. By surfacing and making clear the submerged workings of Whiteness, I believe they might be examined, challenged, and changed. This book does that in three ways: sharing the untold histories and challenging the mythologies of Whiteness and America; critically examining our inherited White antiracist pedagogies; and providing new ways of talking about and working through what it can look like to be a White person who takes up antiracism. We are not only poorly equipped for conversations about race; many of the tools and instincts we have are actually counterproductive. For example, I was surprised to find that more liberal White students had a harder time imagining antiracist possibilities than more conservative White students, and that White privilege ideologies seemed to explain the difference. By taking up new antiracist tools and ways of being, especially new approaches to shame, empathy, trauma, and embodiment, I believe White people can develop confidence and competence in their fight against White supremacy. This book represents my work toward that end. I hope it helps.

In the spring of 2019, I gathered a group of White high school students for a series of interviews and conversations about race and Whiteness. Nine of us met 13 times during the spring of their senior year of high school at St Ann's, the Catholic college prep school in the upper Midwest where I taught English language arts. These participants demonstrated the extraordinary insight and vulnerability of all young people, and whatever insight or clarity I have managed here is largely thanks to them. They will be introduced in Chapter 3. While they represented a range of backgrounds, ideologies, hopes, and anxieties, they shared a level of financial security. They were White people of privilege with broad access to the opportunities of a wealthy school environment, and they knew it. This work, therefore, focuses on the mechanisms of privilege and Whiteness of an elevated financial strata. Whiteness operates within and among White people, sometimes following class lines, so that while all White people share a kind of ancestry, the experiences and perceptions of being White are not monolithic. This is all to say that Whiteness is not a fixed category, and this book does not treat it as one. As will become clear, some of the privilege these young White people worry about is financial, and that is not the case for all White people. Their sense-making about race, therefore, is informed by this.

In the following chapters I work to make sense of my classroom experiences. Chapter 2 chronicles a history of race and Whiteness in the United States, challenging the dominant narrative of a free, equitable country with small racial digressions. This chapter also explores the literature on schooling, goodness, and emotion as they relate to race and Whiteness. This history, alongside my work with goodness and emotion, provides a more helpful framework for understanding what was happening in my classroom. Chapter 3 works through race talk, specifically the patterns of race talk participants shared and described, including how participants understood and critiqued their schooling, available racial discourses, and their own racial discourses. Chapter 4 focuses on participants' underlying racial frameworks, which clarifies how my students positioned themselves. Chapter 5 explores participants' conflicted and fraught emotions around race and race talk, especially the roles of White shame and trauma. This work in particular helped me make sense of the dynamics of my classroom. Chapter 6 works through the emotional dynamics of being White in a White supremacist society. Chapter 7 explores new pedagogies for addressing Whiteness in White-dominant environments, reconsidering what antiracist pedagogy can look like.

Resmaa Menakem (2017) begins his book *My Grandmother's Hands* with a caution, inviting us to pay attention to our bodies as we engage with work on trauma and race, to notice feelings of constriction and thoughts along the lines of, "I'm not like that; I'm a good person" (p. xiii). This caution neatly frames classroom work around race. For White people to effectively approach their own Whiteness, we must engage with a suppressed resistance to examination. Success in this project on Whiteness might feel like failure, like a painful shift out of ourselves. Our antiracist work becomes possible as we permit ourselves to question what goodness means, and to allow ourselves to be vulnerable to these new meanings. Finally, I want to note that however *simple* some of these new ways of being are, I would not count any of them as *easy*. With that, let's begin.

CHAPTER 2

A Brief History of Whiteness and White Supremacy

The more you know of your history, the more liberated you are.

—Maya Angelou

Making sense of the historical context of Whiteness is central to creating a critical White identity. I hope to trace the history of Whiteness in colonial America and the United States to better understand and make sense of its sometimes opaque or slippery workings. I begin with the deployment of Whiteness, an invented social category, as a form of social control in colonial North America and during the tumultuous inception of the United States. Next, I trace the workings of Whiteness through the 19th and early 20th century, where its ambivalent relationship with racial Others[1] shaped and hardened changing performances of White racial identity. I then examine the arbitrary boundaries of Whiteness during the immigration waves of the late 19th and early 20th centuries. My chronology of Whiteness concludes in the postwar United States, when neoliberalism subsumed explicit racism in favor of ideologies that served to obscure and de-historicize this history of Whiteness and race. I examine this through multiple scholarly interpretations. I then review studies on Whiteness in educational contexts, specifically high schools, and conclude with a brief overview of the literature on Whiteness and emotionality.

While Whiteness as a social category doesn't appear until the 17th century, there have long been cultural and moral associations with "black" and "white" within Western ideologies. As far back as the 10th century, names could become "white" and pure again, and tales were populated by fair-haired heroines and raven-haired evil stepmothers (Dyer, 1997, p. 61). Dyer argues for a long-held prejudice against darker colors, including dark-skinned peoples, and these beliefs predate the profound social chasm manufactured as race. On the other

14

hand, while it is nearly impossible to trace the origins of a white/ black dichotomy in the Western imagination, Merlin Stone (1976) has made the case that this binary originates with Hebrew and Christian societies, who deployed them to suppress matriarchal communities. For Stone, the positive view of serpents and fertility figures such as the half-goat half-man Pan were taken up as evil in Hebrew and Christian mythologies to undermine matriarchal authority. In this view, the linking of whiteness with goodness and blackness with evil could be, in part, a function of Western patriarchy rather than an innate human quality. In any case, a thorough review of available scholarship on the topic locates the origin of Whiteness in the tobacco plantations of colonial Virginia.

THE FOUNDATIONS OF WHITENESS

In this section, I trace the foundations of race and Whiteness in colonial America. Whether the origins of race are traced to Portuguese cartographer and historian Gomes Eanes de Zurara in the late 1400s (Kendi, 2016) or to the halls of Virginia's House of Burgesses in the 1600s (Allen, 2012), the heritage of Whiteness is rooted in class tensions and mechanisms of social control. For Kendi, this early mapmaker generated racist depictions of Africans to drive Portugal's nascent African slave trade and please his boss. Allen, meanwhile, traces the origins of Whiteness to the social control exercised over European and African laborers by the economic elite on 17th-century Virginia Company tobacco plantations. I follow his lead.

Colonial Virginia operated as a capitalist free-for-all, with little or no distinction between the wealthy elite and structures of power. A group of around 300 families, in a colony of more than 25,000, voraciously pursued profit from the founding of the colony in 1616 until Bacon's Rebellion in 1687. While the Virginians shared some of the social inheritances of Northern Europe with their counterparts in Massachusetts, the Puritans dedicated themselves to a religious society, rather than to profit. This difference can help explain the comparatively high death rates on the tobacco fields, with nearly half of all arriving European laborers dying while the Virginia Colony became established.

These laborers arrived on hostile shores stripped of both any access to their former livelihoods and any means of creating new ones. They were not allowed to grow their own food, trade with neighboring tribes, or sell their own wares. They were entirely at the mercy of the elite, whose concern for them extended the length of their profit margins. A 5- or 7-year term of indentured labor was often a death sentence for Europeans. In short, indentured workers faced a bleak outlook in the New World. Because these laborers had been criminalized as debtors or thieves back in England, the colonial elite had little reason for sympathy. They padded the accounts of their investors and were celebrated back in London as great men.

Having been enslaved by Portuguese slavers and sold by English pirates, the first African laborers joined the Europeans in 1619. The astronomical death rate, the ongoing and ruthless quest for wealth, and the enormous social gap between European labor and wealth all served to blur any color, language, or religious differences among laborers. We know, based on the laws the European elite later created, that many African laborers were as free as Europeans, and that many came to own livestock and property, including European servants and slaves. We know that African and Europeans married, and that the elite encouraged this to increase their labor force. We also know that colonists changed the centuries-old legal parentage from patrimonial to matrimonial, allowing European men to rape and impregnate African women without losing their access to power (while forbidding any women to do the same).

These exploited workers lived, loved, worked, and celebrated side by side, and aided in each other's periodic escapes. Side by side, in what has become an almost unimaginable class solidarity, they rebelled against their inhumane treatment in Bacon's Rebellion of 1676.[2] Their grievances and resistance flowed freely across differences in skin color. The solidarity among the European and African laborers threatened the existence of the ruling class. This, Allen argues, is where the first vestiges of race, particularly Whiteness, appear. Breaking class solidarity to foster racial solidarity represents the first and central contract of Whiteness.

*   *   *

To better make sense of the mechanism of social control employed by the elite, Allen's analysis begins a century earlier in England, where he explores how the English elite practiced the methods deployed in colonial Virginia. Allen details how landowners, the elite of newly capitalist, 16th-century England sought to remove themselves from the unpleasantness (and danger) of enforcement while maintaining control over their laborers. As English landowners used every means at their disposal, including what was legal, illegal, and not yet illegal, to increase the labor pool and drive down wages, the need for new mechanisms of social control grew urgent. With Machiavellian flair, they elevated members of an emergent middle class, the yeomanry, to stand as a buffer between themselves and the envious masses.

The English yeomanry rose from a class of modest landowners and businessmen. They became moderately prosperous civil servants, and, as overseers of the poor, served to police the newly dispossessed, wage-earning population. When called upon, they would rise to protect their modest corner of the status quo against the landless rabble. Francis Bacon called them "tame hawks for their master, and wild hawks for themselves" (as quoted in Allen, 2012, p. 18). In other words, the English yeomanry served the needs of the wealthy at the expense of the poor in exchange for a modicum of authority and power of their own. Their sense of ownership and entitlement, carefully fostered, informed their social role, so that the English yeomanry believed they acted in their own self-interest. In the aggregate, they protected property and profit over, and often at the expense of, human lives and well-being. The yeomanry of Colonial Virginia served the same purpose, but with one crucial difference: with access to varied skin color, they divided society by creating Whiteness and race.

After the rebellion of African and European laborers nearly succeeded, the elite, dramatically outnumbered as the 1% of the age, sought to disempower the laboring class by targeting their class alliance. The elite directed colonial European laborers to identify as White, like themselves, rather than as economically oppressed. Through a series of laws and policies, they shifted the economic animus of working Whites into a racial animus directed at their African peers, thereby safeguarding their wealth and status. Like their ruling-class counterparts in England, and for similar reasons, the colonial elite enlisted a yeoman class with the same sense of ownership and entitlement.

The Virginia Slave Codes of 1705 systematically advantaged European labor over their African compatriots, dividing the unified working class into White and Black. As one critic protested at the time, they sought to "Afix [sic] a perpetual Brand upon free negroes and mulattos" (Allen, 2012, p. 242). These codes mandated that landless Whites serve in slave patrols, permitted the naked whipping of Blacks (while Whites could be whipped clothed), and seized Black property and redistributed it to the poor Whites. Moreover, in what became a common racist justification, they revised history. By blaming Blacks for their poverty and celebrating Whites for their hard-earned possessions, White people became blameless for and, startlingly, victimized by the suffering of Blacks. America was hardly founded before wealthy Whites complained that neighboring Blacks hurt their property values (Kendi, 2016).

Given token material advantage for their Whiteness and an important affiliation with the wealthy White elite, this White yeomanry embraced their role. By the early 18th century, every county in Virginia had an armed, White slave patrol serving the economic and social needs of the elite. The Virginia planters had successfully divided a proletariat that policed itself by creating something new: race.

Creating a wholly new social category capable of 200 years of chattel slavery and another 150 years of systematic oppression and violence is an extraordinary and horrifying accomplishment. Often, when I have shared this origin story, my White students are shocked at how something so durable was also so incidentally created. "Where do White people come from?" I ask. Their answers vary: Europe? Cold regions of the world? God? That no one was White until the late 17th century, and that those who institutionalized Whiteness did so more out of a self-interest than a deeply held racial animus, unsettles them. Often, their first response is to apply the origin to the solution; that is, if race was so capriciously begun, couldn't we just as easily get rid of it? They miss, and often so do we, that the animating power of racism is not animosity but self-interest, and that self-interest is not so easily addressed.

*   *   *

Strictly forbidden from social exchange with their African peers, these European laborers began forming a racial identity as "White people." Whiteness, loosely helmed by those in the position of acting in their economic interest, continued to uphold the elite by manufacturing and deploying racial differences as an economic foil. In other words, White people came to know themselves as what they were not.

In his history of Whiteness and labor, Roediger (1991) explains how the "prehistory of the white worker begins with the settlers' image of Native Americans" (p. 21). These images initially served to justify land dispossession and contributed to the settlers' image of themselves as "Hardworking whites' in counterpoint to their imagination of Indian styles of life" (p. 21), though in time they came to represent many contradictory values.

Philip Deloria's (1998) *Playing Indian* explores these values in the historical and ongoing formations of Whiteness. Deloria, concerned with how White American men have deployed Indianness throughout history, theorizes two axes on which Indianness existed for Whites. First, White American men made use of Indianness as insiders to imagine deep historical roots on the new continent while later figuring Indians as outsiders and spurious possessors of the land. Second, Indians could be figured as legitimizing, possessing an "authentic" Americanness, or as obstacles, inhibiting modern society. For example, before the revolution, Indians as legitimate insiders served the ruling class intent on fomenting unrest under British rule. Colonists unhappy with logging and hunting restrictions (and later, tea taxes) protested, masked as "White Indians." This soon reversed. After working-class White men won the Revolutionary War for the elites and failed to realize their promised financial standing and property ownership, they again expressed their discontent as White Indians. Only now their interests no longer aligned with those of the ruling class. Elites, for whom the revolution was in the past, responded with images of the outsider, obstacle, "savage" Indian to discredit the protesters and quell this discontent. Later still, Indianness served as legitimizing outsider. White men (and later, women) claimed a lineage to "extinct" Native peoples, claiming artifacts and rituals as symbols of a fictional and deeply hypocritical Indigeneity as they simultaneously engaged in genocide and continent-wide land dispossession of actual Indigenous peoples.

The project of America, in many ways, can only be justified within this hypocritical ambivalence. Generating a uniquely American identity (which is to say White identity) that was *not British* while remaining *not Indian* required it. "There was, quite simply, no way to conceive an American identity without Indians. At the same time, there was no way to make a complete identity while they remained" (Deloria, 1998, p. 37). Playing Indian accommodated both at the cost of locking the ambivalence into place.

Stereotypes do work. They are animated by (and work to assuage) forbidden or suppressed longings and fears. We can only safely confront these stereotypes when we understand the work they do, which is to say when we address those longings and fears. Happily, we must as often embrace longings as confront fears, and what many White people long for are authentic communities and celebrations. Yet we are so organized and divided by race that it can be difficult to imagine communities without these divides. One way to gain access to interracial possibilities is by studying our racial history.

*　　*　　*

In addition to profit-hungry social structures, European Americans brought with them traditions and rituals that served to relieve the pressures of labor and hard living. These included days-long carnivals and feasts featuring an inverted social order, such as a Feast of Fools or a comically elected Boy Bishop. By creating space for revelry, especially mockery, indulgence, and the grotesque, these precapitalist festivals served an essential social function suggested by the common etymology of *revel* and *rebel*. Predictably, revelry met with resistance in the young, profit-hungry United States.

White working-class old world Tammany celebrations, often multiday bacchanals commemorating a fictionalized Indian chief, clashed with elites' need for productivity and discipline, so they "replaced carnivalesque revolution-tinged Indian celebrations with sanctioned holidays in which Indian play transformed the wildness of the Revolution into an obedient patriotism" (Deloria, 1998, p. 68). Further, the newly independent ruling elite secured and justified their control of property by offering, speciously, that poor Whites "held property in [their] own labor" (Thomas Paine, as quoted in Roediger, 1991, p. 45). Without the secure economic footing promised them after the war, working-class Whites struggled to understand their social role and position in the new United States. As the newly White colonists knew themselves by the Blackness they rejected after Bacon's Rebellion, working-class Whites took up, in acceptable and unacceptable ways, the contradictory images of their racial Others. Indianness, foretelling Blackness, became potent with "enormous iconographic flexibility" (Deloria, 1998, p. 29), providing the colonists the canvas on which they would strive to create a new (White) American identity.

Slavery also functioned as a powerful metaphor. Colonial elites, seeking to convince White workers to join the revolution against the British, claimed that the White working class was held in political slavery. Later, slavery was used by wealthy anti-abolitionists who threatened northern White workers with "wage slavery" (Roediger, 1991). The comparison was bimodal; a promise of property and liberty drew White men toward their hopes, while slavery as Blackness, a somewhat tenuous relationship through the last half of the 18th century, drove White men from their fears.

Perhaps the largest missed opportunities for racial solidarity, like the repressed Tammany celebrations, were Black Election Day and Pinkster celebrations. Lott (1995) and Roediger (1991) describe these weeklong celebrations of Black culture celebrated by working-class Whites and Blacks as "a time in which rural and urban populations mixed in cities under black leadership" (Roediger, 1991, p. 102).

Pinkster, the Dutch celebration of Pentecost, was an opportunity for enslaved and free Blacks to socialize, perform carefully satirical jabs at Whiteness, and earn money by singing and dancing. These freedoms (and, importantly, the interracial solidarity they afforded) threatened the tenuous power structure of racial hierarchy. The ruling class regulated and ultimately shut down these celebrations.

In these ways, Whiteness became an identity defined by what it was not. Whiteness took shape by taking on and casting off the partial habits and customs of those who became racial Others, often regulated in the interest of the ruling class. While the ruling class benefited from a subdued and focused workforce, there were profound costs to the people who came to think of themselves as White. By constricting the sanctioned identity play and development of White working-class identities, expressions of solidarity, mockery, ritual transition, celebration, and mourning became masked as Indian societies and Blackface minstrelsy. Whiteness was created and sustained without any understanding of the self beyond the needs of capitalism.

Our contemporary White racial melancholy echoes this disconnectedness. When White people seek to make sense of our role in a landscape populated by the rich and varied cultures of racial Others, we struggle to see beyond the consumption, use, and abuse attendant to capitalism. As I explore in the next section, the White relationship with culture has long been possessive, something to *have* rather than something to *be*.

Ultimately, Indianness and Blackness remained powerful and necessary semiotic tools available to White Americans, as racial historian Eric Lott (1995) summarizes:

> The special achievement of minstrel performers was to have intuited and formalized the white male fascination with the turn to black, which Leslie Fiedler describes this way: "Born theoretically white, we are permitted to pass our childhoods as imaginary Indians, our adolescence as imaginary Negroes, and only then are we expected to settle down to being what we really are: white once more." (p. 53)

WHITE RACIAL AMBIVALENCE, ANXIETY, AND AUTHENTICITY

In this section, I explore the ways Whiteness shifted toward a more formal masking process facilitated by and for White elites. Like Indian play, the singing, dancing, and theatrical performances of Black culture by Black performers were replaced by a fraught institutionalized carnival: Blackface minstrelsy.

In the 1820s, White worker identity hardened through new and established mechanisms of racial representation. Northern White workers desperately distanced themselves from their Black economic counterparts in the South, trading the word *master* for its Dutch translation *boss*, and channeled their economic and social anxieties through Indian and Black masking and identity play. The doubleness of Indian identity appropriation is recognizable in Blackface, where working-class Whites combined an identification with and an aversion to Blacks in Whites' past and labor, a highly ambivalent dualism that persists today. The boundaries of Whiteness, importantly, lived within the tension of this binary of identification and aversion.

For Lott (1995), Blackface performance, racist as it was (and remains), was primarily concerned with the creation and maintenance of White raced and White classed identities. As he argues, "The elements of derision involved in Blackface performance were not so much its *raison d'être* as an attempt to 'master' the power and interest of Black cultural practices it continually developed" (p. 113). Though less central to his study than Roediger's and Allen's, Lott argues that the formation and upkeep of racial ideology have been informed by class anxieties, driven, though by no means controlled, from above by wealthy elites acting in their own economic interest.[3]

Blackface and the models of Whiteness it generated were highly ambivalent. Blackface came to account, through longing masked by ridicule, for specific agrarian behaviors Europeans gave up to become White. Without the outlet of social carnival, minstrel shows provided a sanctioned context wherein northern Whites could engage with what they surrendered through play with Black culture. Lott describes how northern Whites initially encountered Black performers in marketplaces and the carnivalesque election day celebrations mentioned earlier. These modes of Blackness were then commodified and appropriated by White performers who, in Blackface, performed culturally Black songs in minstrel shows; a voyeurism of "the culture of the dispossessed while simultaneously refusing the social legitimacy of its members, a truly American combination of acknowledgement and expropriation" (Lott, 1995, 49). White workers took up the false superiority of racist stereotypes to soothe the loss of having become White. Like Indianness without Indians, White workers attempted to take up Blackness without Blacks. This masked longing can be seen in Irish immigrants singing "Tis Sad to Leabe Our Tater Land," an unsanctioned and unpatriotic nostalgia for their homeland and foregone agrarian lifestyle made permissible through a metaphorical "Blackening" of dialect, tone, and Blackface itself (Lott, 1995).

By appealing to and temporarily satisfying the immigrant longing for a precapitalist, pre-factory culture and lifestyle, minstrel shows articulated and ultimately worked to assuage economic divisions among Whites by deploying racial ones. Whites' tenuous sense of racial superiority mitigated, though could not overcome, discomforting economic anxieties. These ongoing anxieties confronting White wage earners (anxieties they embodied in racist caricatures of Blackness and slavery) obstructed a clear view of all they had lost in becoming White.

*   *   *

Minstrel shows literally performed the interplay between White class anxiety and racial superiority. This social high-wire act demanded precision. Deloria, Lott, and Roediger all note an obsession with authenticity that permeates the identity play of White working-class men, who, having severed ties with their agrarian, autonomous pasts, struggled for cultural footing. As Deloria (1998) wrote, "Because those seeking authenticity have already defined their own state as inauthentic, they easily locate authenticity in the figure of an Other" (p. 101). As mid-19th-century immigrants (Irish, German) celebrated their heritage in Blackface, the social meaning of Whiteness expanded while Blackness became pointed and singular. People becoming White needed specific representations of Blackness because only within and against Blackness could Whiteness see itself. The "authentic" Black American, along with Black culture, was being bought and sold by Whites into stereotypes so durable they came to inform later Black performers themselves. Yet the close association of the Whitening audiences with the Blackness they celebrated and mocked raised the specter of a unified proletariat once again.

The constant threat of Black identity play was the emergence of transracial, class-oriented identification, uniting wage-earning Whites with free and enslaved Blacks against their mutual oppressors. This threat posed by class solidarity, fed by the racial interchange, however tortured, of identity play, was carefully mitigated by the ridicule and fabricated threat of Blackness. By the 1840s, Blackface performances had closed the circuit of longing and aversion, of attraction and revulsion. Performances conspicuously pointed to the dangers posed by freed Blacks to the wages of White workers as well as the threat foreigners posed to republicanism in an effort to secure racial

divisions. Minstrelsy flirted with but could not consolidate racial divides. Interracial class solidarity succumbed to American capitalism,
and not for the last time.

David Roediger (1991) laments the failure of minstrelsy to engage the class unifications that lay just beneath the surface. He won-
ders "how America, for African Americans and working-class Whites,
might have turned out differently if the same social energies and creativity poured into Blackface entertainment had instead gone into
the preservation and elaboration of Negro Election Day?" (p. 127). I,
too, am compelled by the loss of this potential interracial celebration,
which is so unfamiliar to me as to be almost unimaginable. Like those
working-class European immigrants, I feel the strain between my
anxiety over the assurance of wealth, the security from molestation
attendant to Whiteness, and my desire for—what exactly—a festival
I cannot imagine? I struggle so hard to see beyond what I fear losing
that I'm kept from recognizing what I've already lost.

Ultimately, as other race theorists also note, "For White Americans
the racial repressed is by definition retained as a (usually eroticized)
component of fantasy" (Lott, 1995, p. 149). Commonly today, the
White person's initial (or only) encounter with Blackness is to spec-
tate Black athletic or musical performance, where viewing the Black
body "as natural, erotic, sensual and animal" is encouraged (Fanon, as
quoted in Lott, 1995, p. 150).[4] This objectification was generated and
reinforced by the hosts of 19th-century minstrel shows, as well as PT
Barnum's "Freak Shows" (Frost, 2005). Both contextualized a theatrical exchange so that audience, White, was distinct from performers,
non-White. Without Barnum's framing of the "savage" Indians on display, the "White folks" he addressed as such would simply be standing, anticlimactically, in a room with other people. Like Barnum's
audience, Whiteness depends on its observational stance toward racial
Others, without whom it cannot understand itself.

Barnum and the minstrel show hosts, more common in the later
minstrel period of the 1850s–1920s as minstrelsy came under more
official control, named White people as spectators and objectified the
people at whom they paid to gaze.[5] The simultaneous barrier and easy
access represented by the minstrel and freak show hosts serves to other
and exoticize the non-Whiteness on display while tempering the fascination with mockery and control. Again, this importantly managed
the White audiences' identification with and ridicule of the Other.
As the emperor needed his courtiers, Whiteness depended (and continues to depend) on the racial Other (Lensmire, 2018). The flexible

iconography of racial Others on which Whiteness relied served to police the boundaries of Whiteness so that Whiteness remained unsettled into the 20th century.[6]

* * *

Because Whiteness policed the boundaries of power and access throughout American history, Whiteness itself has been a contested space. In this section, I explore the mutable boundaries of Whiteness around the turn of the 20th century. From the late 19th century through World War I, immigrant groups routinely eschewed their ethnic heritage in pursuit of an elusive dream, often vying against each other for access to Whiteness and its socioeconomic advantage. In *Whiteness of a Different Color*, Matthew Frye Jacobson (1998) tracks the sometimes absurd contortions around Whiteness to naturalize as U.S. citizens immigrants from desirable European origins (importantly, there was no process to include or exclude the immigrants themselves until the Immigration Act of 1924).

Through the early 20th century, Italians, Jews, and Eastern and Southern Europeans all straddled the boundary between White and Black. This is evident in legal histories. In one case, a Black man's conviction for miscegenation was overturned in *Rollins v. Alabama* (1922) because of the indeterminacy of the Whiteness of his sexual partner, who was Sicilian (Jacobson). A pair of Supreme Court cases in 1922 and 1923 further demonstrate how arbitrary and variable Whiteness was during this period. In *Ozawa v. United States* (1922), Takao Ozawa sued on the basis of his White skin, claiming the Japanese were "free White people." The court unanimously decided against him, arguing that Whiteness originated in the Caucus region. Yet when Bhagat Signh Thind, himself from Punjab, nearer to the Caucasus mountains than Northern Europe, sued for citizenship in *Thind v. United States* (1923) just 1 year later, the court unanimously ruled that "free White persons" extended to Caucasians "only as that word is popularly understood" (Biewen, 2017). By the early 20th century, the arbitrary boundaries of Whiteness had grown more official and explicit.

My Irish ancestors entered this power struggle when they immigrated in the late 19th century and sought enfranchisement through Whiteness. They were soon joined by immigrants from Eastern Europe, Southern Europe, immigrating Jews, and later Japanese, all of whom were permitted to vie for Whiteness on some level. Confronted with an American nativism that condemned the Irish as bringing with them poorer labor conditions, disease, Catholicism, and other maladies, the Irish chose race over ethnicity and sought to detach themselves from their ethnic past, foreclosing affiliation with the Blackness associated with it in the process. Without a hope of changing Whiteness, the Irish joined up to Whiteness en masse, becoming so enmeshed in their role as yeomanry that the stereotype of the Irish cop[7] and Irish priest persists to this day (I myself come from a rather large family of Irish cops and priests). For them, Whiteness was attainable only by taking up the specific behaviors, attitudes, and discourses of Whiteness. Once inside this exclusive cultural space, looking out with tense disdain at their former comrades, they felt a tenuous safety.

Irish acceptance of Whiteness foretold the modern social and economic mechanisms of White supremacy; access to Whiteness as Americanism was dependent on a relentless repudiation of the humanity of the non-White Other, especially Blacks (Jacobson, 1998; Roediger, 1991). They were told that to be successful they had act like the elite Whites, giving up the churches, foods, and traditions that constituted their ethnic identities. The Irish, like generations of immigrants who followed them, surrendered fundamental parts of their identity (which became celebrated in masked Blackface minstrelsy) for the promise of economic prosperity. The work of Whitening meant shedding an ethnic, authentic past in favor of a racial and racist future. Roediger puts it this way: "The white working class . . . began during its formation to construct an image of the black population as 'other'—as embodying the preindustrial, erotic, careless style of life the white worker hated and longed for" (p. 14). Like the European laborers centuries earlier, this was a catastrophic, immeasurable loss chosen by those immigrants, who then traumatically imposed the loss upon their children. I delve into this loss in the next section.

WHITENESS IN AN AGE OF COLORBLINDNESS

Before I explore the evolution of Whiteness, race, and racism through the 20th and early 21st century, I want to spend a moment extending the theoretical work explored in the previous section in an effort to construct a contemporary psychosocial model of Whiteness. Ralph Ellison, following Du Bois's exploration of the woundedness and paralysis of Whiteness after World War I, explores the great American hypocrisy of liberty fueled by racial subjugation. Ellison (1953/1995) argues that Blackness was placed "outside of the democratic master plan, a human 'natural' resource . . . so that white men could become more human" (p. 85). He names, in other words, the central function of racial stereotypes. Like Du Bois, Ellison recognized the role of Blackness in the American imagination as a necessary counterpoint to understand White accomplishment and failure. Similarly, Toni Morrison (1992) identifies the iconography of Blackness as a "category of imagery, like water, flight, war, birth, religion . . . that make up a writer's kit" (p. x). These writers recognized how identity play provides ground for White Americans to cultivate its mythic understanding of itself. In a sentiment echoed decades later by Whiteness scholars, Ellison sums up the complicated relationship in this way: "Perhaps the object of the stereotype is not so much to crush the Negro as to console the White man" (Ellison, 1953/1995, p. 97). Predictably, and like the Whitening of labor 100 years before, this consolation was achieved at a great psychological cost to the people becoming White. To be sure, this cost in no way compares to or mitigates the great physical, material, and psychological costs the creation and maintenance of Whiteness have inflicted upon people of color, and acknowledging the cost to White people must always be in service to dismantling White supremacy.

Thandeka's (2001) *Learning to Be White* builds on Du Bois, Ellison, and Morrison by locating the origins of the psychic break of White ambivalence (Lensmire, 2017) within children and identifies shame as the potent mechanism by which Whiteness is made. As children who are to become White seek companionship or affiliation across racial lines, they receive negative responses through explicit or implicit disapproval or discomfort, which tells them to remain within their White contexts. For Thandeka, Whiteness is formed by small, personal divestments of the self to remain within the safe social boundaries of family and community. Children "learn to think of themselves as white to stay out of trouble with their caretakers, and stay in the good graces of their peers" (p. 20). These psychic divestments, where children act against their human inclination to exclude those who look different, induce shame. White children then form both an internal and external boundary against race mixing. In this way, Whiteness is sustained by the creation of internal and external non-White zones, made off-limits by a caregiver's disapproval or discomfort. These non-White zones become areas of fascination, a highly ambivalent blending of attraction and revulsion akin to Blackface performers. "The concrete ghetto [and other symbols of Black culture] thus become an objective symbol for both Euro-American's racial fears and her or his desires for a community that does not judge, but embraces difference as good" (p. 26). This loss includes the childlike exuberance of un-self-conscious song, dance, and celebration, a deeply human authenticity. Like the wage-earning Whites of the 1800s, contemporary White children are forced to choose between this authentic humanity and social acceptance. And like wage-earning Whites nearly 200 years earlier, the costs to them are profound.

I argue that this ambivalence in White people manifests in different ways in our modern era of implicit, de facto racism. This era begins shortly after World War II, as I explore next.

WHITENESS AS NONRACIST GOODNESS: NEOLIBERALISM

Racism has long been made tolerable to Whites through selective and deceitful language,[8] but it was not until the dawn of the Cold War that explicit de jure racism became disadvantageous to U.S. leadership, which suddenly found its racisms inconveniently in contrast with its capitalist ideals. Soviet accusations that capitalist United States was fundamentally unequal and the passage of the civil rights laws of the 1960s made explicit racism socially and legally unacceptable. In response, Whiteness took up official antiracisms. Like Whiteness hundreds of years earlier, racism was made ahistorical, so that the United States became innocent to its cause and, brazenly, "victimized" by accusations of racism. Melamed (2011) argues that we are now within "a formally antiracist, liberal-capitalist modernity that revises, partners with, and exceeds the capacities of White Supremacy without replacing or ending it" (pp. 6–7). In this model, the solution to racist treatment lay in assimilationism, where people of color needed only eschew their deficit-laden culture and become White, as generations of European immigrants had done.[9] Specifically, the 1965 Moynihan Report, which claimed that a collapse of Black family structures (not ongoing racism) was responsible for racial disparities, was taken up by many White people as a liberal antiracist cause. Here, alongside the modern, good, nonracist White person, with all of their well-meaning and good intentions, "the genocidal sincerity of false empathy" was modernized (Vaught, 2017, p. 133).

While de jure racisms named White supremacy explicitly, through the now-condemned mechanisms of colonialism and genocide (Mills, 1997), these overt racisms have been replaced with de facto racism, wherein, "because the discrimination is latent, [it is] usually unobservable, even to the person experiencing it" (p. 75). Because these de facto racisms function within a purportedly equal society, our *"failure to ask certain questions"* helps secure what Mills calls the "Racial

Contract," which has now *"written itself out of formal existence"* (p. 73, emphasis in original). In this way, the Racial Contract seeks to narrow our understanding of racism so that we can only recognize it in the past and as isolated aberrations, rather than in our taken-for-granted social systems.

Moreover, with "racism as status quo" (Mills, 1997, p. 76), and by locating racism within individual attitudes and identities, good nonracist White people systemically underestimate the potency of present-day racism in relation to past racism, and fundamentally misunderstand the mechanisms of racism and racist social policy. Reinforced by neo-liberal ideologies of fierce individualism and Melamed's (2011) "official antiracisms" disseminated in "race novels" from *Uncle Tom's Cabin* (Stowe, 1851) through *The Help* (Taylor, 2011), racism is popularly understood as discriminatory actions from individual persons or companies, for which that individual can confess, atone, and be welcomed back into good nonracist Whiteness (Lensmire et al., 2013). It is these individual bad actors who, official antiracism holds, maliciously generate racist policies to create inequality. The reality is the opposite, as Kendi (2016) argues: "Hate and ignorance have not driven the history of racist ideas in America. Racist policies have driven the history of racist ideas in America" (p. 9). Good, nonracist White people are complicit in misunderstanding these systems, allowing and, in many cases, encouraging them.

It is hard to overstate how normal, how ubiquitous, how commonplace and commonsense good White nonracism is. Good White nonracism reassures good White people of their goodness in books and movies with clearly demarcated heroes and villains, and in true crime stories with the law on "our" side. The dream is comfortable houses far from "dangerous" neighborhoods; it is growing savings accounts and appreciating home values. It is our faith in the criminal justice system, the police, the attorneys, and the prison system, working to put behind bars people who deserve to be there. It is our trust in the electoral process, a government that is looking out for our best interest, or one we can safely ignore. It is Coates's (2015) dream in *Between the World and Me*: "It is Memorial Day cookouts, block associations, and driveways. The Dream is tree houses and the Cub Scouts. The Dream smells like peppermint but tastes like strawberry shortcake" (p. 11). The "Dream" is the rotten heart of nonracism, innocently tucked into good nonracist Whiteness.

When we fail to recognize the roots of our contemporary support of our legal and economic systems in the historical context of the legal and economic conventions of racism, we can dangerously misrecognize both our history and ourselves. This misrecognition allows us to simultaneously condemn the legal structures of slavery, Jim Crow, and poll taxes while upholding contemporary legal structures of policing, incarceration, and voter disenfranchisement. White people tend to believe that the good White nonracism of today is somehow different from that of our history. We miss that, as I will detail later, the legal racism of our colonial past was upheld by good White nonracists. Our racial ideologies, while differing in meaningful ways from the racial ideologies from history, ideologies we might recognize as racist or even foolish, are foundationally the same.

Like Kendi, Mills (1997) argues that White America fundamentally misunderstands race in part by stubbornly believing that racism is *not* normal. His case is devastating and worth quoting at length:

> Racism and racially structured discrimination have not been *deviations* from the norm, they have *been* the norm. . . . the Racial Contract creates a *racialized* moral psychology. Whites will then act in racist ways *while* thinking of themselves as acting morally. In other words, they will experience genuine cognitive difficulties in recognizing certain behaviors *as* racist, so that quite apart from questions of motivation and bad faith they will be morally handicapped simply from a conceptual point of view in seeing and doing the right thing. (p. 93, emphasis in original)

History was not made by bad racists and good antiracists only. The bad racists depicted in books and movies have been the exception; the lion's share of our society's racisms have been upheld by good *non*racist whites, while the *anti*racists of history have been marginalized as extremists (Malcolm X) or watered down to White-acceptable shadows of their radical selves (Dr. Martin Luther King). By critically examining nationalist formations, we can uncover the justifications that generated, sustained, and insulated the long and surprisingly consistent history of good White nonracism.

WHITENESS, GOODNESS, AND THE STATUS QUO

Most historical atrocities were committed in the name of the law, and our own are no different. Some of our most potent and damaging forms of contemporary racism are exercised in the name of being a good American. Saving and investing hard-earned money is the hallmark of good American Whiteness. The good nonracist White people of the 1820s, much like today, were concerned with the financial return on their investments. Like today, they invented and commodified profitable securities based on financially stable mortgages, now called mortgage-backed securities. Like today, they deregulated these instruments and saw speculation take off. These securities allowed investors across the world to greedily build strong returns for nearly a decade before the entire structure, massively overleveraged, collapsed into a national economic panic with significant global implications, most severely punishing the poor and racial minorities. Whites similarly directed their anger at White elites, minorities, and domestic foreigners (Baptist, 2014, Kendi, 2016). The only difference between the mortgage-backed securities collapse in 1837 and the one in 2008 was the property being mortgaged: houses in 2008, Black bodies in 1837. In both instances, the assumption of a racially neutral financial system allowed good nonracist Whites to invest without a concern for racial impact. It was self-interest with acceptable consequences.

Additionally, American governmental programs of social uplift have, from the beginning, distributed this aid in blatantly racist ways. From the Virginia Slave Codes in 1705 to the New Deal and the GI Bill, which "gave birth to the White middle class and widened the economic gap between the races, a growing disparity racists blamed on poor Black fiscal habits" (Kendi, 2016, p. 358), to farm insurance claims today (Biewen, 2017), all scrupulously directed financial benefits to Whites and away from Blacks. As in history, the action is erased so that Whites are celebrated for their hard work and Blacks are then blamed in racist terms as lazy, incompetent, and immoral for their inferior economic conditions. With a supposedly impartial socioeconomic structure in place, racists and nonracists alike looked for answers to the question of racial disparities. Rather than question the structures themselves as antiracists have, racists and nonracists each found their answer, at least in part, in the deficiency of Black people. Large parts of moderate and conservative political platforms (cutting taxes and social programs) rely on and perpetuate this myth (Haney López, 2013). Heather McGhee's (2021) *The Sum of Us: How Racism Costs Everyone and How We Can Prosper Together* explores the harm these policies cause to the White communities who support them.

Finally, good, nonracist White people can ignore the recent history of sunset clauses and redlining and blithely accept that living in segregated neighborhoods is a consequence, however regrettable, of an impersonal market rather than their choice to participate in and benefit from the long history of economic discrimination. I say this as a person who owns property in one of the most liberal and most White neighborhoods in Minneapolis. These structures are deeply entrenched in our social fabric and identities, which make them difficult to interrupt.

The argument here is to make more recognizable those who profited from slavery, not the slave drivers themselves, or the Georgia men who traded them domestically, but the northern and European financiers who were doing their level best to make money just like the rest of us. Baptist's (2014) central argument is that racism and slavery not only profoundly shaped American capitalism but that racism *remains* deeply implicated in our economy. Michelle Alexander's 2012 takedown of the 13th Amendment outlawing slavery except as punishment for a crime, *The New Jim Crow*, helps us recognize the ongoing financial exploitation of people of color, especially Black men. Companies like Wal-Mart, Starbucks, McDonald's, and Sprint profiting from the use of prison labor in 2020 (Shabazz, n.d.) reflects the decades-long practice of Jim Crow. Even without imprisoning Black folks, racist policing practices, such as in Ferguson, Missouri, in the 2010s, have been designed to excessively fine Black residents to generate income for the municipality, as determined by a 2016 U.S. Justice Department, Civil Rights Division (2015) investigation. These policies were not hatched as racist fantasies. They were economically expedient with consequences that were deemed acceptable.

Being a good nonracist White person, then and now, means believing and investing in the state and state economy as an instrument of good, or at the worst neutrality, while sustaining an ignorance of their racist lineages. It means believing in the inherent goodness of American education, which remains largely unquestioned. For good nonracist White people, the achievement gap is attributed to cultural deficiencies, or, more charitably, to individual students, and occasionally teachers, as though a national opportunity gap between White students and students of color can be located in the classroom. Indeed, calling it the "achievement gap" (rather than, say, the opportunity gap) implicates the achievement of individuals or cultures, rather than implicating an educational system that has never in its history equitably addressed the learning needs of students of color.

WHITENESS AND THE RACIAL CONTRACT

In addition to the socioemotional struggle that teachers and young people experience in classroom education about Whiteness, there are also sociocultural constructs that work to thwart young White people's close examination of race and racism. White people are insulated from the experiences of people of color through Western epistemologies that favor specific ways of knowing. Vivian May's (2015) *Pursuing Intersectionality* offers a useful tool kit for unpacking these hegemonic ideologies. May explains how, in situations of inequality, dominant ideologies generate "an agreement to know the world wrongly" (p. 190), which then limits available meanings and values to those of the dominant group, while disregarding "the interpretation, reception, and overall perception of knowledges generated by disenfranchised groups" (p. 208). For White people, this means that non-White experiences, especially of racism, become not only difficult to see for White people, but that White people "gain an 'immunity' to stories and evidence not corresponding to established ideas" (Code, as quoted in May, 2015, p. 191). This has led well-intentioned White people to declare an abstract acknowledgement of racial discrimination with only a limited ability to see it. May (2015) further explains, "The exclusions and erasures embedded in the universal are obscured by an array of knowledge conventions, state practices, and political norms that mask or render illegible these bald-faced contradictions" (p. 192). It is precisely these "knowledge conventions, state practices, and political norms" that constitute a "racialized moral psychology" that antiracist pedagogues must address.

These racial norms May explored confound what it means to be a good White person and to live a moral White life. Charles Mills (1997) conceptualizes these norms as a Racial Contract, into which good White people invest themselves as members of the American social order. The Racial Contract normalizes racial inequality by obscuring its genealogy so that contemporary racial disparities can be understood as temporary and exceptional, rather than historical and by design. The contract also renders visible inequalities acceptable by "establishing personhood and subpersonhood" (Mills, 1997, p. 53), where unequal social treatment of those deemed subpersons is rationalized and accepted. One way to make sense of our long history of White supremacy recognizes the role of nonracism, wherein self-interest generates racial inequities and is celebrated as White goodness. The project of Whiteness ignores this history, what historian Lewis Gordon called "a cult of forgetfulness on a national scale" wherein "the more the racist plays the game of evasion, the more estranged he will make himself from his 'inferiors' and the more he will sink into the world that is required to maintain this evasion" (as quoted in Mills, 1997, p. 98).

White people, because of the knowledges, practices, and norms of Whiteness, will struggle to even recognize normative systems of racism, much less divest themselves from them. Recognition of racism, to say nothing of divestment from racism, will take intentional, personal, and sustained work. Throughout our history, and still today, it has been possible to be a good nonracist White person while socially, emotionally, and financially investing in brutally dehumanizing beliefs, instruments, and institutions. It is possible to blame Blackness as deficient while denouncing the centuries of ongoing oppression. As Frederick Douglass said: "When men [*sic*] oppress their fellow men, the oppressor ever finds, in the character of the oppressed, a full justification for his oppression" (Kendi, 2016, p. 199). Each of these challenges must be named, unpacked, and processed to productively address race.

NEOLIBERALISM, CRITICAL RACE THEORY, AND WHITE PRIVILEGE PEDAGOGY

As neoliberalism seeks to individualize and "unburden" economics from the human systems that give our economy shape and meaning, critical race theory (CRT) counters by recognizing the human racial biases that inform and define these systems. Originating as legal scholarship in response to the shortcomings of the civil rights movement, CRT prioritizes the experiences of people of color to recognize the insidious and often unrecognizable effects of racial oppression. Rather than presuming racial liberalism, as neoliberalism demands, CRT works toward racial literacy by bearing witness to the profound, systemic, and ongoing impact of race on our society and systems of education (Gay & Kirkland, 2003; Ladson-Billings & Tate, 1995). CRT works to address Mills's moral handicap experienced by White Americans and provides the theoretical foundation for the following critiques of three common White responses to race talk: colorblindness, colormuteness, and color celebrating.

In a colorblind society, as Bonilla-Silva (2014) writes, "whites rationalize minorities' contemporary status as the product of market dynamics, naturally occurring phenomenon, and blacks' imputed cultural limitations" (p. 2). Colorblindness, "the problematic conflation of race with racism that reinforces inequalities, hierarchies, and racial division while insisting that race does not matter" (Roberts et al., 2008, p. 337), is the racial hallmark of neoliberalism. Colorblindness implies that noticing race, not racism, is the problem. This becomes especially dangerous when Whites identify as race-less. One way people of color seem to present a racial problem to White people is simply existing in certain spaces; noticing people of color can fly in the face of colorblindness. As I explore in Chapter 3, colorblind ideology is central to the racial sense-making of White people, even those who recognize its flaws.

Likewise, in *Colormute* Mica Pollock (2004) explored how, in addition to purporting to not see race, we strenuously avoid talking about race. This can lead to a maze of rules about race talk, including that "people do and do not belong to simple racial categorizations," and that "race does and does not matter" (pp. 13–14). Yet when schools attempt to enact race-neutral policies, White ideologies about classroom structure, discipline, and academic achievement are treated as normal, inform policies, and reinforce racial hierarchies. With Whiteness both implicit and invisible, nonracist schools are confounded by the inevitable racial gaps. Like colorblindness, colormuteness is a neoliberal maneuver intended to inoculate a White person against accusations of racism.[10] How can the school be racist with clear policies that forbid racism?

Building on CRT, WPP sought to address these White maneuvers. WPP (White privilege pedagogy) has been dominated by McIntosh's (1988) model of White privilege, the "Invisible Knapsack," where White people are meant to understand their Whiteness as a set of unearned privileges, unknowingly carried around with them. Because of the predominance of the "Invisible Knapsack," race talk in high school classrooms has often been limited to a debate over the existence and importance of White privilege. In other words, WPP often functioned as an unproductive rhetorical debate among anxious White people without providing them with the resources to move beyond it (Lensmire et al., 2013). I argue that WPP is the dominant racial discourse within which young White people make sense of race, race talk, and themselves as racial and moral beings.

WHITENESS AND SCHOOLING

There has not been a great deal written about Whiteness in high school despite the call of Black American authors such as Dubois, Ellison, Baldwin, and Morrison to do so (Lewis & Diamond, 2015). Further, the literature that does exist on Whiteness and high schools seldom contends with the history of Whiteness detailed previously. Contemporary Whiteness studies, especially those focusing on high school settings, have rarely addressed Whiteness using historical and emotional under-standings of Whiteness. Moreover, commonsense structures of race, including multiculturalism, race as something one *has*, and race avoid-ance through colorblindness and colormuteness, leave schools woe-fully underprepared and even counter-prepared to contend with race.

Most work on Whiteness and race in high school does not root it's theory of race or Whiteness in a historical context, focusing in-stead on "how and why race mattered" in their research context (Lewis & Diamond, 2015, p. 4). While much of the literature notes the shortcomings of recent scholarship on Whiteness (Bucholtz, 2011; Perry, 2002; Trainor, 2008), by failing to consider historical origins of Whiteness and Whiteness studies, they miss and misattribute foun-dational theoretical work (including DuBois, 1995; Morrison, 1992; and Thandeka, 2001). The authors note the functions and superficial social origins of Whiteness and race but do not trace or historically locate these attitudes, many of which developed to serve the explicitly racial purpose they purport to uncover. For example, Matias (2012) calls for, but does not complicate, placing the burden of race on White people without a reckoning of how that burden has functioned his-torically. A knowledge of the violence enacted by working-class White men against bodies of color *in response to* historical burdens, includ-ing lynchings, racial violence during the economic downturn of 1837 and the Draft Riots of 1863, would appropriately caution against cel-ebrating a burdened White masculinity. Further, now that Whiteness can be taken up explicitly, publicly, and in profoundly negative ways, what young White people do with that burden can be dangerous. The history of Whiteness is relevant for these reasons.

What most of these studies miss, and what Trainor (2008) names, is that few White high school students attend to the power structures in which they are privileged (access to accelerated courses, parental financial access, lack of official surveillance), while they closely attend to the more salient social power structures in which students of color *are* in positions of power, including constructs of toughness, coolness, and dominant musical and stylistic modes. As Trainor (2008) put it, "Students do not appreciate the systemic nature of privilege because they do not experience privilege systemically" (p. 135). Social capital in high school *can* be distributed in favor of students of color, especially in the eyes of socially marginalized White students, and this discrep-ancy can inform White resistance to antiracisms. Having reframed the mechanisms of racism, we can assume resistant White students want social parity with their peers of color. As Trainor points out, failing to recognize the sincere desire for camaraderie in White students' claims such as "my ancestors never owned slaves," leaves us without the emotional tools for unpacking such sentiments (p. 25).

The resistance of White students can be more productively understood as originating outside of the protective or possessive stance to which it is commonly attributed (Lensmire et al., 2013; Trainor, 2008). When presented with the false dichotomy of confessing privilege or being racist, some White students reasonably protest. These are students who might lack ethno-racial pride and are targeted for their Whiteness regardless. Trainor's proposal, that some aspects of racism originate in misapplied emotionally held beliefs rather than racial animosity, offers new antiracist approaches.

By focusing on emotion and persuasion, Trainor (2008) reconsiders the racist discourses of high school students. "I began to see that the persuasive power of racist discourses cannot be explained by what is generally understood as racism—that is, negative attitudes or feelings toward non-White people arising from ignorance, lack of empathy, or a desire to maintain race privileges" (p. 23). Her interest in the origins, rather than examples, of racist thinking gave her new insight into why high school students remain unpersuaded by antiracist thinking. She identifies a number of schooling processes that contribute to racist beliefs, particularly official notions of what racism means, what she calls the "misapplication of emotionally held beliefs" (p. 5). For example, defining racism as discrimination based on race can lead to a host of problematic discourses, including colorblindness, White racial victimhood, and reverse racism. This can also support the rejection of antiracist ideologies, especially identifying CRT as discriminatory.

Trainor (2008) lists common school "rules" embedded in the official antiracisms of multiculturalism, alongside their unintended consequences for antiracist work:

1. Rule: we have to respect everyone the way they are
   Unintended Consequence: don't change the way I am
2. Rule: be cheerful!
   Unintended Consequence: don't bring me down with your social justice
3. Rule: conversation means debate, which requires open-mindedness
   Unintended Consequence: everyone is entitled to their equally valid opinion, and every conversation has two equal and opposite sides (p. 89)

As she points out, it is difficult to be both morally outraged and open-minded about racism. Trainor also describes a familiar pattern in which students resist antiracist discourses by "overextending the rules of tolerance" (p. 113). In other words, they employ a Whitewashed, individualistic multiculturalism in place of a critical systemic perspective in order to claim a kind of immunity to accusations of racism. Teachers and students are thus limited to understanding racisms as situational exclusion and discrimination based on race. Rather, as she suggests, "We need to see student racism as a mediated emotioned phenomenon that emerges from and responds to the routines and culture of schooling" (p. 102). In other words, student resistance is more about who they sit with at lunch than a considered social ideology.

All of these studies offered similar sets of classroom and schoolwide practices to combat the racial risks inherent in Whiteness, including an awareness of youth culture, surfacing race in official discourses (Bucholtz, 2011; Perry, 2002; Pollock, 2004; Thomas, 2015), encouraging complex considerations of race and identity, and fostering communities of difference, what Fine et al. call "equal status contact theory" (as quoted in Perry, 2002, p. 197). Another common takeaway was that racism was informed by a "feedback loop . . . whereby social structures and stereotypes of different youth-influenced behaviors that, in turn, reinforced or 'proved' the need for racialized social structures and the veracity of the racial stereotype" (Perry, 2002, p. 176). Further, the literature cautions that we must sensitize ourselves to the possibility that we may *think* we are supporting diversity while we are working against it (Lewis & Diamond, 2015; Mills, 1997). These strategies hold. Yet, with the added dimension of Trainor's emotioned perspective, we have two added cautions:

1. "Addressing such students will require getting beyond metaphors that equate White racial identity with tangible assets and moving toward seeing Whiteness as a series of ongoing emotioned strategies and negotiations—as a process" (p. 139).
2. Echoing critical Whiteness theory, we need to move beyond the "real time racism" model of catching students saying and doing racist things (p. 15).

Contrary to the suggestions of Thomas (2015) and Thompson (2003), this is not work that can productively happen online or as "debate."

Nor will racism "be ameliorated by increasing White students' exposure to difference" through multiculturalism (Trainor, 2008, p. 139). Nor is the work without risks.

THE IMPACT OF THESE CHALLENGES ON CLASSROOM CONVERSATIONS ABOUT RACE

In addition to concerns of hardening young White people against race talk or promoting ineffective models of White shame or guilt, taking up race in the classroom raises its own concerns. First, for White students to confront race, they must "give up the notion of themselves unproblematically as good whites," which can feel deeply threatening to those taught from an early age that being racist is one of the very worst things to be (Thompson, as quoted in Ambrosio, 2014, p. 1379). Due to this threat, White students often resist antiracism and antiracist pedagogy, which positions them as racist, and will undertake logical and emotional countermeasures to protect themselves. In addition to colorblindness, colormuteness, and color celebration explored in Chapter 3, these countermeasures are informed by the models of Whiteness mentioned and can include the following:

1. Deploying a fatalistic guilt or a scapegoating blame, "problematic binaries" of extremes that forestall conversation (Ambrosio, 2014, p. 1385)
2. Heavily qualified agreement with antiracism, or deploying the force of facts—however cherry-picked (Ambrosio, 2014)
3. A "past-future orientation" to racism, which avoids calls for action in the present (Kendi, 2016, p. 361)
4. What Applebaum (2016) called White silence,[11] the result "when white students are exposed to the insidiousness of whiteness and when pedagogy interrogates white ignorance and white innocence" (p. 389)

Importantly, we can understand White silence in multiple ways. For example, Gaertner and Dovidio theorized "aversive racism," a classroom practice where students are so loathe to commit an "unwitting transgression that could be attributed by themselves or by others to racial antipathy" that the risk of censure outweighs the moral right and they refuse to speak at all (as quoted in Ambrosio, 2014, p. 1386). Classroom teachers and theorists both commonly read White silence as resistance. However, I believe we can productively read the silence as one of many forms of "stuckness" inherent to race talk in predominantly liberal White classrooms, which I explore in Chapter 6. The deeply laid causes of these reactions to race talk, particularly racial shame, lie beyond the view of most high school teachers (who are overwhelmingly White). These complex reactions from students often become flattened to "resistance" so as to fit within teachers' confessional models of antiracism.

That is an intimidating catalogue of the workings of Whiteness. I am cautioned not only by these theories, but also the personal pedagogical experiences I detailed in Chapter 1. I might, in a moment of recognition like this, invite some deep breaths and openness to address any constricted feeling in my chest and shoulders. I remember Menakem's invitation to introspection from the end of Chapter 1, to spend time with my personal resistances and stuckness. I must periodically examine how I remain invested in structures that cause harm, otherwise I risk dismissing potentially liberatory criticisms and frameworks in deference to a temporary comfort. The dream Coates identifies as poison offers me a great deal and is not so easily set aside, and however helpful new models of Whiteness may be, they are not always easily taken up. My resistances happen in my body and are persuasive. By periodically pausing, breathing, reflecting, and creating openness, I can work to prevent my White body from derailing my antiracist work.

Personally and pedagogically, I now take up Whiteness in new ways, informed by the historical process of Whitening and armed with an understanding of the White epistemologies that serve to protect Whiteness. Like Kenney (2000), "I needed to teach myself to see that which I had been trained not to notice. I needed to pay attention when my own anthropological questions met with resistance" (p. 122). As a classroom teacher, I sought to better understand how these new perspectives might advance my understanding of the resistances of young White people.

As a whole, our understanding of young White people remains constrained by superficial understandings of Whiteness too often informed by neoliberalism and McIntosh's privilege model. Current literature on Whiteness in education has provided a nuanced set of observations, skillful descriptions of how young White people act, with only a few probing more deeply into making sense of White emotional states, including Trainor (2008) and Matias (2016).

CONCLUSION

This historical perspective makes possible understandings of the workings of Whiteness that can serve to better make sense of the experiences and behaviors of young White people. The dynamics of Whiteness described in each historical period continue to "work," making each essential for a deeper understanding of what it means to be White today. Further, thanks to more recent scholarship it is possible to complicate our understanding of Whiteness in helpful ways. I brought these new understandings of Whiteness to bear on my work, as I explore in the following chapters.

CHAPTER 3

Race Talk in School

It's ok to talk about it. And it's something we should be talking about. I feel like it is something we should talk about.

—Maria, January 11, 2019 (personal interview)

Race talk in high school is a tense performance of Whiteness at the confluence of historical, national, and local discourses, wherein young White people must navigate the strict morality of WPP (White privilege pedagogy) using the purposefully deficient language of neoliberalism. Young White people are both authentically caught and authentically experiencing pain within Whiteness, so any potential antiracism requires unpacking their experiences of Whiteness and race. Before going on, I want to acknowledge that whatever suffering White people experience due to White supremacy does not compare with or mitigate the ways White supremacy has harmed people of color in both individual and systemic ways over hundreds of years. Addressing the negative impacts of White supremacy on White people must never lose sight of that.

Young White people can feel bound within the discourse formed by neoliberalism and WPP, which afford, broadly speaking, three possible positionalities. The first is colorblindness, "the problematic conflation of race with racism that reinforces inequalities, hierarchies, and racial division while insisting that race does not matter" (Roberts et al., 2008, p. 337). The second is White guilt and shame, a function of the confessional model described in Chapter 2. White racial trauma, which the Reverend Thandeka (2001) describes as childhood familial threat when White children cross unspoken racial boundaries, complicates shame and guilt, creating emotional binds that are explored in Chapter 6. Jennifer Trainor (2002), in her study of emotion and race in education, describes the binds this way:

Student responses to the constructions of whiteness encountered in their texts and, in turn, their own constructions of whiteness were rhetorically delimited in problematic ways by an essentialized whiteness that critical pedagogy, sometimes unwittingly, set in motion. (p. 641)

A third possibility, White ethno-nationalism, has been increasingly taken up by disaffected Whites who have been encouraged to blame racial and ethnic minorities for the economic fallout from neoliberalism. Race scholar Charles Gallagher presciently worried that White people might begin to take up Whiteness as "an explicit carrier of group interests," in 1997. The election of Donald Trump was only the latest stage in this resurgence of White ethno-nationalism. This third option alone speaks to the need for effective antiracist pedagogical intervention and support.

As a caution, these are not distinct ways of being. Rather, as I will explore, these identities overlapped, where an expression of White guilt might coincide with colorblind attitudes. White ethno-nationalism, being explicitly counter to both colorblindness and White guilt and shame, did not figure into my work. However, as an aggrieved and resistant identity, I am reminded of the relative safety of colorblindness and cautioned about the importance of movement and new possibilities beyond shame and guilt. Ultimately, the WPP model of race and racism dominated the race talk of these young White people.

PARTICIPANTS

While I did not ask about political affiliation as part of my initial interview protocol, most participants used a liberal-to-conservative binary to assess the racial views of themselves and peers. I'll follow this binary here.[1] Roughly speaking, more liberal equated with more concern for race and racism, what Frankenberg (1993) calls "race cognizance," while more conservative meant a more neoliberal, individualist, bootstrap narrative view, with little consideration of social contexts. With these in mind, I attempted to enroll White participants with a range of beliefs about race, with little success. Prior to our time together, the women participants, Jenny, Heidi, Maria, and Ali, had all articulated racism as serious problem, a more liberal view. Of the young men, Ben was the only participant I was confident held more liberal views. I knew that Joel, Ryan, and David had shared skepticism of systemic inequalities, more conservative views, in class the year prior. I was unsure of the views of Ken and Danny.

Importantly, Ken, Ryan, and David all shared how they had shifted their views from last year so that they were now more aligned with those who believed racism was a serious problem. David actually apologized for what he had shared with me during an interview last year, while Ken, who has soft eyes and a wry smile, told me how he "used to be majorly Republican and now I'm more liberal, I care about more people." Without Joel's participation in the group meetings, the ideological diversity of my participant group was limited to "liberal" views.

I want to take a moment to introduce Joel. While his absence allowed for a critical examination of the presumed sameness of participants' racial ideologies, it was also a loss. His initial interview, the only time we spoke "on the record," was rich and fundamental to my sense-making of emotion. Joel is an attractive kid, soft brown eyes, a likeness of a young heartthrob. I remember seeing his profile during the interview and thinking he could be a movie star—he would never be held back by his appearance. There was something in his good looks that threw me, as I noted after our conversation in my field notes:

> He wore a leather jacket over a gray hoodie. His clothes, shoes, haircut, and face all looked expensive to me. He had a knowing half-smile I've suspected before, a smile that caught a teacher instinct of mine, is he up to something? It's a hard feeling to shake, particularly when he espouses conservative notions of White male victimhood, which seem to require an almost cult-like adhesion of a set of beliefs at odds with reality. Having known him for 2 years I still can't quite shake it—when he smiles at me inviting him to participate, when he smiles at a question . . .

I will note, emphatically, that my descriptions of White male victimhood are about me. In fact, it is certainly possible to read his mysterious smile as an anticipatory reaction to the way I would write about it. He knew me as well as I knew him (or likely better than, given our unequal statuses in the building).

The remaining nine participants demonstrated dynamics within liberal antiracist discourses that I take up later in this and the following chapters. That participants held more liberal views (as well as Joel's limited participation) was likely conditioned by the topic of our conversations; potential participants could self-select out if they felt that their views would conflict with the political zeitgeist of the enrolled group. Indeed, one potential participant and two enrollees asked who else would participate, and several participants suggested that having friends in the group was a contributing factor in their participation and candor. I examine their suppressed reckoning with their roles as young White people in a White supremacist society by beginning with the linguistic elements of participants' experience of race talk.

REFERENTIAL LANGUAGE

The discourses of race talk available within schooling profoundly influenced participants' available ways of understanding race, racism, and themselves. I begin with an overview of the language participants employed to talk about race both because of the discursive baseline provided by such an examination and to highlight the central role language, or, in this case, the lack thereof, plays in our sense-making about race. For this discussion, I use the phrase referential language to include the words or phrases participants used to describe or refer to race, racial issues, or racial identities.

Participants all expressed concern and confusion about how they were to undertake race talk, down to the language they would use to refer to concepts, groups of people, and individuals. We discussed how to define terms such as race, racism, and Whiteness in our sixth meeting. After a few participants named race as socially constructed and appearance based in what felt like rehearsed and school-sanctioned language, Ben pushed his fine sandy hair out of his face and observed, "I think it's intentional . . . the fact that we may struggle to answer that question is evident of how we're not really given a language to talk about race." Ali, her arms and legs crossed, then demonstrated this difficulty in a way that resonated with the rest of us:

> *Ali:* Um, adding onto that, I, well for all of these it's kind of hard to like put into words because like, I've never, I don't know, either. I think about it, like what is the right way to say it or what's the right way to think it? I guess? I don't know if there is a right way but . . .
>
> *Kevin:* If there's a right one, I want to know what it is and then I'm gonna use it. Is that what you . . .
>
> *Ali:* Yeah, I could—I don't even know if there is a right way of, I mean, there's a wrong way.
>
> *Kevin:* What's that?
>
> *Ali:* Um, I don't, I don't really know [laughter].

Ironically, Ali is articulating a difficulty many White people encounter when attempting to talk about race, which is that White people are eager to say the right thing without knowing what that is, and desperately fear saying the wrong thing without knowing exactly what that is either. In our final conversation she shared a similar feeling of having *always already failed* at antiracism: "I mean like would you [have] said like there's always something more to be done? There's always that like, you know when you like leave and you forget something, like you know when you need to go on a trip and you're like, I forgot something. It's kind of like that to me." Ali wore her brown hair bobbed. Her head was often slightly lowered, which gave her an air of always leaning forward. Her contribution here was characteristic of her other comments and of WPP; racism must be dealt with and there's no "good" way to do so. White people both *must* participate in race talk and *do not know how* to participate in race talk. It extended to the seemingly simple task of talking about people in racial terms.

Perhaps as a consequence of this, there seemed to be a consensus among participants that the term *African American*, more ethnic than racial, felt safer than the term *Black*. Heidi, more sure of herself than most, mentioned that she might revert to using African American when she was unsure. At the same time, she also struggled to find the right language:

Jenny: I don't know, I feel like growing up it was just implied that you say African American instead of Black, but like now I don't really know if that's entirely accurate.
Heidi: Because I've been like, because I totally get what you're saying Jenny, I feel like mostly like in school and life, just like my everyday life growing up people were like, oh, African American like that's, like a respectful term you should use. But now I feel like I've heard um, African Americans say that they prefer to be called Black. Like I've heard people say like I'm Black so call me Black. So that's where I'm like, okay, like I don't want to like offend anyone by saying African American if they'd rather be called Black, but I don't want to call someone Black if they'd rather be called African American.

Similarly, Joel described why he felt he ought to use African American by naming "the feeling in society that you have to stay away from using words like Black." Yet while African American seemed safer, Jenny noted how White people don't "call ourselves Caucasian American," and Ben complicated the use of "Black" by noting that context and emphasis could render the word as derogatory or not. David provided the only nonessentialized definition of what "race" or "Whiteness" might mean, reminding us that there are as many ways to be "Black" as there are people who identify as Black.

Furthermore, attempting to avoid the term *Black* can be taken up in confusing ways. For example, Ryan referred to Black South Africans as "African American" twice in our initial conversation; he sheepishly corrected himself both times. In my own anxiety to get it right, I'm guilty of this slip myself. The anxiety over the language used to refer to racial groups can itself predominate race talk well before antiracism can be taken up and can lead to counterproductive performances of antiracism among White people.

David was the only participant who didn't seem close to anyone else in the group. He brought a sincere intellectual curiosity to race talk; he spent time on Twitter following and listening to commentary about race. In our initial interview, he described how reading accounts of sexual harassment and assault online had changed his views on gender and feminism. I failed to ask what shaped those early views on gender and feminism, but I suspect they also came from the internet. David's fingers were always moving, picking invisible pills from his sweatshirt cuffs. His restless eyes contributed to his nervous look, and he spoke with an almost imperceptible lisp. He wore an analog watch on a plastic band. David was the only participant who seemed willing to directly contradict the ideologies of WPP. For example, I believe he correctly identifies the performative nature of the referential language we use:

> *David:* Well, and this might be a bit of a, I don't know, maybe controversial, maybe not, but I think that the term *African American* is more used by White people than anyone else. It's, I—yet again, I would say like maybe they're trying to be, you're trying to sound more virtuous, or you know, woke, by trying to be overly, you know, respectful to that.
>
> *Ben:* They're overcompensating for something.
>
> *David:* Yeah.
>
> *Maria:* That kind of makes sense.

Because sense-making happens in large part through language, the lack of a coherent discourse around race limits participants' capacity to understand not only race itself, but also their place within racial discourses. Unable to confidently put language to racial topics, these young White people were left with little recourse but to either hide in silence and shame or anxiously perform antiracism through calling out. Calling out, as explored in Chapter 4, is often a consequence of White privilege pedagogy.

Moreover, because neoliberal education in high school is typically classroom bound and oriented toward efficiency, students' only available action is through language, often limited to the pedagogical language of the teacher (Freire, 2007). This leaves confessing to privilege or calling out other White people as the only antiracist actions available to young White people. It can seem like the only thing to do in a classroom is talk, and there is not adequate language. I believe this language problem is foundational to the rest of the participants' racial discourses.

SCHOOLING

Schooling, the formal education these young people encountered in their mostly Catholic elementary schools and St Ann's, was for the participants a nearly universal disappointment when it came to race. The group provided clear examples of curricular and pedagogical failings. Many noted how their teachers had filibustered race talk "conversations," posed broad questions ill-suited to conversation, or noted how these conversations were entirely and sometimes conspicuously absent. Ryan summed up these shortcomings this way:

> In elementary school when you first learn about race, you learn about MLK and other civil rights people, you're automatically assumed you're not racist. And that's that. There's no education about what race is. So you're saying, "Okay, good. You're in 2019 and you're not racist, now go into the world." So you have no idea about racism or about race and have no handle on how to go about it.

Ryan was tall, even when seated, and had long elegant fingers that moved with his constant hand gestures. He was soft-spoken, and his words seemed to catch in the front of his mouth. He had been skeptical of WPP, and while he now wanted to get smarter about race, he was keenly aware of the stifling effects of classroom discourses on race and anxious about making mistakes. For example, he observed how "you still see in a high school classroom, people are scared of, White people are scared to talk about race, fundamentally frightened."

There were several specific ways in which participants' schooling impacted their race talk. Importantly, participants noted that race talk in nearly all schooling contexts went emotionally and sometimes pedagogically unsupported. Many participants described early academic encounters with racism as witnessing physical violence inflicted upon Black bodies, typically in the 5th or 6th grade. This included images and videos of horrific violence that "disturbed" and "shocked" them, with one participant describing a scene as "scarred into my brain." Sadly, this also seemed to be these White students' primary encounter with bodies of color. Participants were also deeply affected by more banal instances of oppression; Ben described an image of a plantation owners' spreadsheet listing the values of human beings that shocked him.

In addition to these exposures, their high school teachers allowed limited space for discussing race. These moments were often in response to controversial current events involving police brutality and Black Lives Matter protests, where the conversation became heated exchanges among the same few passionate students. In this way, much of these White students' encounters with race talk in any form looked like violent imagery and conflicted, tense arguments with no opportunity to emotionally process these encounters. Participants emphatically noted the lack of follow-up conversations in school, among their peers, or at home.

The lack of socioemotional support for young people encountering racism, even young White people encountering it in an academic context, seems to have significant and far-reaching consequences. Not only did participants evince a kind of stuckness within race talk, as I explore in Chapter 5, but the abrupt context in which race as a topic had been shared seemed to resonate with participants beyond their personal understandings of the subject. For one example, participants noted that these early encounters almost seemed designed to dissuade them from talking about race. As Ben observed, "We're not given a language to talk about this. That's one of the reasons that the problem persists because we don't know how to talk about it. The institutions that would give us the language to talk about it don't have a vested interest in dismantling that system." And, from Jenny, "It was always interesting, just the fact that we don't know how to talk about it is just like a testament to what it is." In contrast to David and Ryan, Jenny made slow, self-possessed movements, as if she could remain perfectly still. She wore her straight strawberry blonde hair at her shoulders and spoke insightfully about race talk. She continued, "Cause it's interesting, how everyone like claims to want to get there. But then it's like if we are on board, how do we get there? And if, if we're going to be talking about the same thing, I don't know. Yeah. It's just like, I feel like I've never had a conversation like that before."

These encounters also aligned with how many participants seemed to understand the nature of race talk itself. Because schooling frequently used historical violence to impress upon students the importance and severity of racism, students seemed to link racism with physical violence, while potentially unlinking it from economic or structural racist violence. For example, Maris's 5th-grade teacher censored a film of police violence against civil rights protestors. I asked her what that was like for her:

> I mean, [shifts in her seat] I mean at the time, I guess I didn't really think much of it, just because like the entire movie was hard to watch already. So I mean, part of me, like, I guess I was like okay with it, but like I guess it just shows the reality that there's much worse things going on, then, that we weren't allowed to see happening.

Maria was a self-professed theater kid, with a clear voice and expressive face. In fact, she came to her racial consciousness in theater spaces where she was exposed to racial injustices during the show *Twilight Los Angeles*. As she told me, "I think being exposed to that when I was 14 has made it, has made me want to know more rather than, just like, still continuing to just skip it over. And not talk about it, I guess." Maria's response to her teacher skipping graphic moments of police brutality shows her discomfort with having turned away from that violence, as though the only way a White person can appreciate racism is to bear direct witness to its physical brutality. Similarly, Heidi was characteristically critical of her schooling for failing to adequately educate her about the civil rights movement. "I feel like if we actually talked about it in school and not just like, 'Yeah, like here are all these great people from the civil rights movement.' No, like, they should talk about the brutalities of it too."

For both Maria and Heidi, their cross-racial encounters, at least in the context of race talk, must look like encountering images of violence and suffering to be legitimate. These encounters positioned the White students as spectators, taking in, evaluating, and then feeling bad on behalf of those suffering. As a teacher I facilitated these encounters, providing my students with what I hoped were convincing examples of racism. I am both sympathetic to Maria's guilt at being allowed to look away and responsible for the limited way Heidi understood these encounters. Schooling has problematically called for them to feel empathy for the oppressed. I take up the empathetic relationship in Chapters 6 and 7.

Further, the stuckness of race talk is rooted in schooling that presents racism in primarily historical terms. In the same way high school students struggle to understand Nazi-era Germany with nuance and sensitivity, uncomplicated White supremacy becomes overexposed and cartoonish. Racism is then limited to the more extreme portrayals of violence and unambiguous prejudice seen in films like *The Help* (Taylor, 2011), *Django Unchained* (Sher & Tarantino, 2012), and *Hidden Figures* (Gigliotti & Melfi, 2016).[2] White students have little choice but to identify with the uncomplicated White hero, leaving unexamined the ambivalences inherent to Whiteness and antiracism. There is no conversation to be had other than a spectator's awe and empathy, neither of which serve as a call to action.

Additionally, one of the ways participants seemed to relieve their discomforting sense of responsibility was to blame their schooling. Participants criticized their schooling for not teaching material early enough, or because schooling didn't provide enough analysis. However, their academic history sometimes contradicted that criticism. For example, Heidi mentioned that she watched the movie *Selma* (DuVernay, 2014), which depicted that violence, as a senior in school. Jenny shared with me that at her predominantly White Catholic grade school "we had waited so long to learn about Malcolm X" in the 7th grade, having studied Martin Luther King 2 years earlier in 5th grade. When I asked participants if they had learned about red-lining, several were quick to say that they hadn't *until* high school, as though by then it was too late. Additionally, in a small group meeting, Ali, Heidi, and David shared a somewhat rare and gleeful moment of ideological alignment by bashing their formal education on race. For example, on the racist war on drugs, David shared, "I think I learned like at the very basics of it [the racist war on drugs] from school, but I learned most of it on my own," and from Ali, "I learned that in Spectrum.[3] I, I wasn't taught that at all before."

Similarly, David seemed to insist that race was not covered well even while encountering experiences where it might have been; ultimately, he argues that if race is covered, it must be "forced":

> I mean obvi- yeah, like in my history class we talked- it was again like bare bones. Like it was, it didn't go deep. It was just 'Yeah, that happened.' . . .

I think I took APUSH [AP US History] and obviously there we had to know like, why it happened, so I think—it seems unless it was forced I, we, it didn't really get mentioned.

At the same time, that participants had encountered these topics in the course of their studies complicates their claim. This demonstrates that truncated pedagogies about race and the lack of processing conversations both suggest, as participants noted critically, a model where racism looks like interpersonal violence located primarily in the past, disconnected (admittedly, like much of schooling itself) from our present lives. However, rather than believe that schooling considers racism undeserving of personal examination, participants were eager to note how their teachers and schooling itself had failed them by conspicuously avoiding the topic. Effectively, they recognized and were critical of neoliberal ideologies within their schooling while expressing similar ideologies themselves, as noted in the following section.

Finally, the structure of schooling itself, as has often been noted by critical education theorists (Britzman, 1991; Trainor, 2008; Vaught, 2017), discourages the kind of analytical thought required to address complex problems like systemic oppression. These particular shortcomings were also not lost on participants. As Ben observed, "I feel like I've spent the last 12 years of my life sitting in a room thinking, spent with very brief periods of actually doing." Maria shared a similar critique:

I mean, with slavery it's like "Oh, they're written into the constitution now, they have the right to vote [false bright voice] and it's better!" and, um, civil rights, like, "they were protesting and things were, it was like, bad. But then, you know, they have more rights, [false bright voice] so it's okay!"

Maria's criticism highlights the dangerous effect of pedagogy homogenized and divided into discrete units. More dispiriting perhaps was the passivity she evinced in our final conversation, which I attribute, at least in part, to the structure of schooling itself:

It's really funny because in my head I was like, I *hope* this conversation continues or I *hope* it's something that's going to continue because I know I'm graduating within 10 days. Yeah. So I was just *hoping* that in the future it's something that it *continues to be brought up*. (emphasis added)

Maria's sense of dependency over her hypothetical official curricula to address race, rather than, say, raising the topic herself in any context, demonstrates her boundedness to official notions of race talk and lack of imaginative capacity to see beyond it.

In summary, schooling was understood to be not enough, perhaps never enough. The excited agreement among Heidi, Ali, and David seemed aimed at self-exoneration, at least in part, by positioning themselves as knowers despite their schooling. They attributed their shortcomings or missteps, not inappropriately, to their deficient education. In an environment focused on unit-sized "problems" within discrete subject areas, important topics like racism can appear to be impossibly complex, which is how some participants talked about race. If antiracism means taking up action, the traditional structures of schooling binds students as passive consumers of knowledge who mostly listen and only sometimes talk, with little or no control over curricula. The dynamics of these conversations can also problematically fall into commonsense patterns, such as valuing differing arguments equally, as I take up in the following section.

BOTH SIDES-ISM

Nearly every participant expressed a desire for what they called "deeper" conversations about race, both within their classrooms and in our conversations together. I pursued this several times before coming to understand that "deeper" suggested a desire to have a dialogue with both sides where students not only felt free to say what they want to say, but where they actively disagreed. For Ali, deeper conversations about race involved "being a little uncomfortable." It also seemed to encompass a desire to hear from peers in an environment that decenters teachers' voices, for example, "I feel like it's been very, I'm taught at, instead of learning with, others." Importantly, it meant a belief that a better understanding lies between differing views. This is congruent with a Hegelian (read: Western) understanding of knowledge production where "unbiased" and "neutral" mean the synthesis of two opposing perspectives, as though the truth lay halfway between a fact and a lie, and that a conversation without debate or disagreement leads to facile or incomplete conclusions. Ken explained it this way:

> I just feel like disagreement brings like better ideas into the frame. It defi-
> nitely opens up people's minds because if one person disagrees, someone
> else is gonna either agree or disagree, and then we'll have, eventually

we'll come to an understanding of what we think it is and probably a stronger understanding than just, Oh yeah, I agree with you.

Heidi shared a similar sentiment: "I value diversity in thinking, in how people think, I don't think productive conversations can happen unless there's push-back, or like, you hear from different perspectives or different sides."

This belief was also taken up in meeting 5, when David referenced the music video for "I'm Not Racist" (Lucas, 2017). He described the song and video this way:

> A Black guy and a White guy sit down at a table and they're super stereotyped with both sides. . . . I felt like that's a, that would have, would for me be like a really good deep conversation with you to talk about both sides of it.

Heidi agreed, though both were careful to note that, as Heidi said, "I think there's definitely problems on both sides that need to be addressed. But I don't know. I feel, I don't know, I feel like White people are more at fault, like have more problems that need to be addressed." Similarly, in her initial interview, Heidi criticized Black Lives Matter while positioning herself as being interested in both sides:

> I don't understand what it means to be a person of color. So like I don't want to—like it's just like what we were talking about I don't want to sound like I'm attacking Black people for saying this, but it seems like— like I said, it just seems like both sides are so resistant sometimes. And if both sides, like if White people would recognize that there actually is an issue. But I feel like—like, people of color, recognize that there are some people trying to help, and I think that they do, but I think and that's where it's difficult, it's that there's such a front to both sides.

In both instances Heidi pushes back against what Margolin (2015) called "the myth of equivalency," where "both sides" implies two *equal* sides. This, however, felt secondary, and did not preclude her calls for movement from both sides.

There are different ways to make sense of this desire to debate and challenge perspectives that participants described. Its effect has been pervasive in my own pedagogical attempts at race talk where racism and antiracism somehow stand equally matched in a detached, logical consideration of people's lives, as though justice lay between harm and an attempt to address that harm. This democratization of morality might be the inevitable result of intellectualizing race, of moving race out of reality and into the sterile classroom where rules like "fairness" and logic, rather than complex social identities, govern sense-making. In "Rethinking Racism," Jennifer Trainor (2008) explores how unspoken rules of schooling, such as needing to maintain a positive attitude, or what constitutes fairness, can have unintended consequences in terms of how students think about race and racism. I believe calling for both sides of a conversation about race could be an example of this slippage. It could also reflect a desire for more authentic engagement in race talk with their peers, where they have access to less bounded conversation. I take up this second possibility in Chapter 6.

However, the fundamental concern with both sides-ism is the insidious common sense of dominance and hegemony, which carry a comforting familiarity and an assurance of safety. Colorblindness remains a deeply persuasive model of race talk. Guinier (2004) describes its rise this way: "In the 1950s prejudice was understood as an aberration in individuals who disregard relevant information, rely on stereotypes, and act thoughtlessly. Prejudice was a function of ignorance. Educated people, it was assumed, are not prejudiced" (p. 116). Roughly speaking, CRT, in an effort to surface persistent racisms that recognize and explain systemic racial inequality, responds to the erasure of race by presuming the significance of race in all social encounters. As I explore in the next section, even White people on the watch for colorblindness carry its ideology with them. Ali was right to recognize the productive discomfort of pushing beyond these ideologies.

Ideological diversity can be a strength. Yet taking up "both sides" of an issue subject to hegemonic pressures, such as race, inevitably skews in favor of the dominant "side" (Kincheloe & McLaren, 2005). As long as schooling continues to assert, as does St Ann's in many cases, that we must consider all sides of an issue or conflict, students from dominant groups will have access to the discursive safety of dominant, oppressive ideological regimes in the name of "fairness." Critical pedagogy is oriented to elevating the voices of the marginalized, not equal recognition (Kumashiro, 2002). While at least some participants recognized the inherent inequality of race, this group of young White people, despite their progressive attitudes toward Whiteness and race, remain subject to this view. In other words, participants' stated understanding of systemic power structures did not prevent them from believing in a "fairness" that called for people of color to meet them halfway.[4] Participants were also caught in commonsense discourses of neoliberalism, as explored next.

COLORBLIND, COLORMUTE, AND COLOR CELEBRATE

Perhaps obviously, a forbidden topic of conversation doesn't disappear, it submerges. CRT and much of the subsequent scholarship and sense-making on race has attempted to work through the ways race talk operates through coded language and omissions. Coded race talk, a function of Whiteness, lives *just* beneath the surface of our conversations. In a colorblind environment, noticing race, much less naming it out loud, violates the individualist neoliberal norms wherein a good nonracist person "doesn't see race" (Bonilla-Silva & Forman, 2000, p. 52). Because noticing race contradicts this ethos of nonracism, colorblindness has complicated the act of referring to a group of people. Despite this group's embrace of race as a topic requiring conversation, participants evinced considerable anxiety around how to talk about it, as explored earlier, and were not immune to the pressures of colorblindness.

While only two participants openly embraced a colorblind view, several shared anxieties about recognizing racial difference, and almost all used coded language at some point. Mica Pollock (2004) called this being "colormute." For example, Ali struggled with whether to recognize racial difference and what that meant:

> Um, I mean when I, I mean . . . when I go to work it's more diverse and . . . I, I have, I sometimes catch myself thinking about it, but like I usually don't think about, "Oh I am talking to someone who is Hispanic or I'm talking to someone that is Black," like it's just kind of like talking to another person.

For Heidi, encountering race explicitly caused her discomfort:

> And it was kind of *funny* just because it's like these 2nd graders doing this art project, but now that I'm thinking about this it, it kind of makes sense, but it would be like, "Jamari is the color of chocolates" or "Skye is the color of a peach" . . . to me it kind of seemed, it just seemed a little *weird*. (emphasis added)

Of the participants, Heidi was the most vocal about the need to address race and racism directly; she read DiAngelo's (2018) *White Fragility* as a choice book, she talked about being a vocal advocate for WPP and called out her peers, and she was the most outspoken participant. Still, she was thrown, at least initially, by an age-appropriate activity designed to name difference in positive ways. Like Heidi, several participants used words like *weird* to describe a situation in which race played an uncomfortable or indeterminate but important role, describing neighborhood segregation or academic differences as "odd," "weird," and "interesting." In his initial interview, Danny used "odd" or "weird" a dozen times; for example, when talking about different areas of his neighborhood, he told me, "My mom has a rule you can't go past there. Like, you can't go there past 10 o'clock at night, because it is, it's weird," or "depending on where you go it can get a little odd." What is happening here? That Danny's "odd" or "weird" could be indexed as class (or, really, anything), complicating any effort to make sense of what he means, is the point. Within neoliberal colorblindness, racial discourses can remain veiled even within conversations about Whiteness where we focus directly on race.

Additionally, several participants hesitated to notice how racism manifested in their experience of tracked schooling lives, where students are divided into honors and regular courses in ways that often reproduce or magnify racist social effects, by telling me that what they were about to say "sounds bad." A passage from my initial interview with David typifies this and is worth quoting at length:

> *David:* I only had a couple classes that were not full of like, I guess, White kids, cause it was either White kids or Hmong kids in my class. Because . . . this sounds really bad when I say it. Because I took like, a lot of the, uh, I guess African American[5] students were more like . . . this sounds really bad I know, but they didn't take like, the super like, high-level classes like, my parents forced me into. So whenever I was in, like, super high-level classes it was just White kids and Hmong kids.
>
> *Kevin:* Yeah. Why do you—like, what's, what's happening when you say that? You say "it sounds bad" . . .
>
> *David:* Yeah, it sounds bad. Because I'm not trying to say like, you know, they couldn't do it, or that, but like, I mean it's not like there wasn't any—there definitely was, but yeah. It just—it sounds kinda weird to say that like, they didn't want to be there or something. I don't know.
>
> *Kevin:* Well, I mean, you're just describing what was happening, right?
>
> *David:* Yeah.

> *Kevin:* Like there was—these were the kids in the advanced
>   classes, and these are the kids who weren't, and you noticed
>   that there was a racial aspect to that. And I don't hear you
>   saying anything like "Oh they couldn't" or whatever.
> *David:* Yeah.
> *Kevin:* But it sounds like you're—you were just kind of nervous
>   about saying that? Or hesitant 'cause you didn't want it to
>   sound wrong?
> *David:* Well it's 'cause I think there is sort of that stigma that, that
>   you know, that they can't do that or something. Or if—I
>   suppose that's probably what I was saying, what I was going
>   to say. If there isn't like one particular group of people in sort
>   of a, a higher place, not, not saying that like an advanced
>   class is like a higher power, or anything, but in like a higher-
>   up place than, you know, there's obviously something wrong
>   going on if there isn't, if a particular group, if not everyone is
>   represented in a particular group.

As David notes at the end, there *is* "obviously something wrong going on," and he demonstrated, as all participants demonstrated, a clear recognition of some systemic inequities, if not a functional understanding of their role in it or its impact. Yet here, and in similar passages from Heidi and Danny, participants struggled to articulate that these disparities are due to systemic racism and, perhaps for fear of saying the wrong thing, or of sounding racist, they hesitated to name them at all. For Thandeka (2001), non-White zones are areas of shame; to enter and name them is meant to be shameful (a function of neoliberalism to discourage White folks from accidentally encountering their Whiteness). Participants' coding their race talk, therefore, is not devious or even intentionally self-preserving. Coding follows the unspoken rules of Whiteness. I believe these young White people (and the rest of us White people), code their race talk in spite of themselves, and that struggle to name Whiteness and race is central to our embodied antiracist practice. Perhaps part of the function of the shame-based White privilege pedagogy is to, through confession, accommodate and move that shame.

However, my initial interview with Joel suggests what might be another tension within participants' race talk. After telling me that I "might not like" his statement, he described how there are not many Black kids in his advanced classes. I asked about his hesitation:

> *Joel:* Kinda fits the stereotype. Um, the kids who are Asian and
>   took, their parents put forth the money and the kids were

> willing to sacrifice their friends and all that to come here for a year and really like push through, are in these high-level classes [he slows here], and I don't see the same thing coming from Black kids. Um . . .
>
> *Kevin:* So you noticed that, which I've also noticed. I think most people have noticed it, but you seem . . .
>
> *Joel:* But you can't actually say it.
>
> *Kevin:* Well, yeah, what's that about?
>
> *Joel:* When a stereotype, uh, comes true, people don't want to hear it.

I wonder if part of David's and others' hesitation to name these racial stereotypes is anxiety about how others might read the racial disparities they identify. Joel seemed anxious that I would censure him as racist for articulating what was, for him, a kind of truth about race, while David seemed anxious that his observation would be read as that same racist truth even as he took great pains to clarify that that was not what he meant. As Bonilla-Silva (2014) argues, colorblindness conflates race with racism, forestalling the very conversation necessary to dismantle the impacts of systemic racism. In this case, not only are participants anxious to identify racial disparities for fear of saying the wrong thing, they might also fear contributing to the racist misreading of social disparities by their peers. Part of antiracist work in education looks like imagining multiple motivations in any moment of race talk, not only to permit a young person the benefit of the doubt, but also to recognize the complex system within which race talk takes place.

Finally, DiAngelo's (2018) work on the defensive and insulating functions of colorblindness and what she calls "color celebrate" were both apparent in participants' race talk. Color celebrate, a more "progressive" position, was more evident within this group than colorblindness. Participants seemed to go out of their way to describe these interracial interactions positively. For example, "Like it's such a diverse school and it's, *I think it's really cool* (Heidi); "Um, they talk about their culture a lot, *which I think is cool* because it's, it's mostly Hispanic. I think it's, it's interesting to learn about" (Ali); "I was pretty good friends with one of the kids there. . . . A couple of them were ethnically diverse[6] and *I felt like I was good friends with them*" (Ken, emphasis added).

For DiAngelo, these linguistic maneuvers served to protect the speaker from racial reproach; as in, "How could I be racist? I celebrate diversity." I agree with this reading, though I want to be cautious about any sense of superiority, more woke than, that might attend this or any other identification of the workings of Whiteness. We tend to think of justice work in terms of progress, as if the journey is a single path moving forward. As if the evasiveness of celebrating color as a White person is not the same evasiveness I attempt in a dozen other ways. Locating myself ahead of or better than anyone else, however White they are, is still White supremacy. Even some kinds of anger at the stuckness of other White people can be rooted in that colonizer's "better-than" mentality. Antiracism is a practice of deepening our understanding of ourselves as raced people, which is cyclical, lifelong work.

For the participants, given Joel's reading of racial disparities, I wonder how much of the care with which they refer to people of color and racial topics is not self-preserving signaling so much as responding to or forestalling potentially racist attitudes of their peers (or themselves!). There were only rare moments where participant conversation did not show a heightened sensitivity and unease, moments that, incidentally, often included laughter. The exact causes of their sensitivity and unease deserve consideration beyond self-preservation.

These are also moments to invite openness, to pause and create space. Whenever our students (or ourselves!) share or demonstrate a discomfort with antiracism can be an invitation to reflect and check in with our bodies. These young White people's evasive language is not intended to be devious; rather, their uncertain language is evidence of their discomfort. As such, it is an opportunity to explore, with them, what they are evading and why.

BEYOND SELF-PRESERVATION

In addition to the race-evasive concerns attendant to colorblindness and color celebration, these moments demonstrate the pervasive anxiety White people experience when talking about race, and little wonder. White race talk, rightfully under scrutiny after four centuries of racial oppression, is fraught with landmines, significantly landmines enforced through calling out by anxious White peers, as I explore in the next chapter. However, participants seemed attuned not only to the landmines themselves, but also to the race-evasive moves their peers have employed to protect themselves. For example, during one of our group conversations David prefaced a comment about conversations with his friends in this way: "I've had plenty of discussions with a lot of, I've—this sounds so dumb to say, I have a lot of [he gestures air quotes] Black friends, but you know what I mean [laughter]; we do find it very entertaining." Incidentally, in our final conversation, David referred to these linguistic maneuvers, such as "I have a Black friend," as "race deflective," a noteworthy insight in itself.

This is a good moment to observe that participants and I laughed together, and occasionally we laughed a lot. Sometimes, like in the previous example, we laughed at the overwrought dynamics of race talk, though we mostly laughed at ourselves. We joked in that meeting about how the Subaru (the car I drove) was the car of woke White people, and how David with all of his "Black friends" might want to look into getting one. In another meeting we joked about the hashtag #basicwhitegirl (which is mostly about all things pumpkin) and the difference between dad jokes and Whiteness. I worked to create space for laughter by example, the same way I worked to create space for other forms of race talk. Because most race talk lives on the margins of acceptable discourse, laughter can help emerge the discussion from being submerged within codes, or from what Lensmire (2017) called "basement culture." I believe our self-effacing and White-effacing laughter created space for more serious conversations that would not have been possible without it. There are a range of possible White identities beyond WPP's resistance and confession. The identity of White people does not live within a binary, and there is antiracist potential among all those identities. My mistake, being limited to and misunderstanding the functions of Whiteness as resistance and confession, severely constrained the antiracist possibilities of my classroom work. I explore the antiracist possibilities of a complexified Whiteness in Chapter 6.

While much of participants' race talk sounded like the conversation recorded by other Whiteness scholars (Perry, 2002; Trainor, 2008), some of these discursive maneuvers (including humor) did not align with recent scholarship about Whiteness. Importantly, David's consciousness about White discourses of "Black friends" complicates Matias's (2016) argument that such a claim is a colorblind defense used by good White people. Additionally, not once did participants explicitly celebrate the profession of White privileges as "signs of courage, selflessness, benevolence, and honesty," as argued by Margolin (2015, p. 8). Perhaps, because the participants were uniformly interested in working against racism, their White privilege was understood, taken for granted. In fact, participant introductions took on a kind of ironic self-awareness. Ken picked up on this by introducing himself as though he were at a self-help group, pausing for recognition (and laughter) after saying, "Hi, my name is Ken, and I'm White." Participants seemed not only less beholden to the less generative constructs of Whiteness proposed by Matias (2016) and Margolin (2015), but familiar enough with them to use them for laughs.

Further, Matias (2016) argues that Whites sometimes take up a facile antiracism by asking what they can do as a way to assuage their guilt and perform their goodness, as in "I feel bad after hearing what I heard and thus want to prove to everyone I am a good person" (p. 70). For Matias the question isn't authentic. While these participants struggled to articulate antiracist actions, they did not seem to perform their Whiteness in this way. Nor did they take up counter knowledge, what Matias describes as questioning the lack of education on race, as a nascent antiracism. Rather, participants joked about how inadequately they had been prepared. Like their White privilege, that their schooling had misled them was assumed.

There remained significant overlap among participants' statements on race and recent scholarship on Whiteness. For example, Margolin (2015) highlights a need not only for "cognition," which the White participants clearly demonstrated, but also the "motivation" to surrender their Whiteness, which several participants argued was lacking (e.g., Heidi, David). What my work demonstrates is not that young White people are no longer subject to the fraught ambivalences described by Whiteness scholars, but that some are highly sensitive and occasionally resistant to these ambivalences, however bound they remained by them. Whiteness is not about simply "being" or "knowing"; it is about navigating complex, contradictory, and highly emotional discourses, and often several at the same time.

Margolin (2015) closes by noting, "[Whites] need a reason to give up so effective a way to publicly proclaim, without penalty, how good it is to be white" (p. 8) (i.e., through a confession of White privilege. I believe Margolin's critique of White privilege pedagogy is well justified, as WPP "misunderstands White privilege as a cause rather than an effect of white supremacy" [Lensmire, 2018, p. xii]). I do not propose that the young White people with whom I worked are not subject to the machinations of White supremacy. However, their ironic self-awareness signals a need for new understandings of the workings of Whiteness. While Margolin (2015) touches on a powerful dynamic within Whiteness here, I believe she misattributes the self-affirmation of "how good it is" to be White to Whiteness as a confessed identity. Rather, my data and analysis show that high school students' goodness resides not only in performing Whiteness directly through confession, but in performing Whiteness through calling out, through a kind of performative[7] antiracism: a White, anti-White, antiracism—a Whiteness through wokeness. I take up these ambivalent maneuvers in the next chapter.

CONCLUSION

As expected, there is no shortage of interrelated and contradictory issues with which to contend, and these are only a sampling of potential constructs and models of high school race talk. Progressing from language, which underlay the race talk in our conversations, I provided examples of how participants discussed their experience of schooling, including both sides-ism and the strained discourses of colorblindness, colormuteness, and color celebrating. I noted how participants both demonstrated and challenged scholarship around Whiteness. Specifically, participants articulated sophisticated understandings of racial discourses, however bound they remained by them. To further explore how participants participate in and comment on these discourses, I shift my focus toward how young White people perform antiracism through calling out, beginning with how an individualized understanding of racism leads young White people to locate racism within individuals, including themselves.

CHAPTER 4

Antiracist (Im)Possibilities

When you are brought up in a White suburb [laughter], you're taught to believe that anyone, all races, can pull their bootstraps. 'Cause the people living there are the very few minorities that were able to do that.

—Ryan (personal interview, April 30, 2019)

The previous chapter addressed the intersections of racial ideologies with participants' schooling. Recognizing that each topic overlaps with the next, and that any categorization has limitations, this chapter shifts to the impacts of other racial ideologies, in particular how individualism fosters counterproductive performances of antiracism in calling out in/out groupings within Whiteness. In this next section I explore the persistent role played by individualism, the deeply American belief that we succeed or fail according to our merits. Participants stubbornly maintained these views, seemingly without recognizing it. Stories from David, Ryan, and Maria set this up.

INDIVIDUALISM

As neoliberalism shifts attention away from de jure structural racial practices, race, in addition to racism, becomes located within individuals. There were several ways participants demonstrated an individualized understanding of race and racism. David's understanding of the systemic nature of racism was typical of the group. I asked, for example, if he struggled with internalized racist stereotypes of Black people. He responded, "Well, I mean, of course. Like, that's like, just a part of, uh, like, media and peers and all this stuff like crammed in there over the years, so obviously it's there, but it's just like, uh, you just gotta ignore it. Just be like—just treat 'em like a normal person." He also shared individualistic views of race, such as colorblindness. "One of my, I guess main beliefs in that sort of situation is just, the golden rule essentially. With race, like, treat everyone like humans unless they give you some reason to not like them."

David, like other participants, demonstrated some understanding of systemic racism and White supremacy, yet individualism dominated his and other participants' understandings of race. For example, participants recognized how local property taxes generate unequal funding for public schools, yet their understanding of racism, even within school, was more commonly understood to be personally injurious and emotional. This second example can be seen in participants' concepts of antiracism, which seemed limited to interpersonal interventions. For example, "I haven't been put in a situation where I feel like I've had to do anything yet" (Ali). Or one participant's belief that claiming his nonracism was enough: "I keep pushing the idea that 'I'm not racist, I promise.' Like I don't want to be labeled as that" (Ken).

Additionally, rather than recognizing structural inequality as the progenitor of race and racism, Ryan and David both described racism using a contagion metaphor, wherein racism spreads interpersonally like a disease: "All it takes is one person to find something about like some civil war, civil rights movement and it's one person to say I think I'm better than you. And then it starts all over again" (David). Even though participants expressed an abstract awareness of systemic racism, these understandings seemed muted by individualist perspectives when it came to concrete examples of racism and antiracist possibilities.

Finally, individualism seemed to position White people as ignorant about race because of their Whiteness. For example, several participants voiced concerns about discussing race among White people. As Heidi put it, "It's not supposed to be a conversation with just White people because White people don't experience racism." That White people might *perpetuate* racism, and thus be implicated in the topic didn't seem to apply.

Maria shared a related story about how her participation in a conversation about racism with people of color was limited to listening, which gets at the complicated interplay of individualism and Whiteness:

I've had a couple [of conversations on race]. It hasn't been in a classroom setting, it's been more casual. It was in the costume room[1] . . . and we were listening to, I say listen because there's really not much that I can, there's really not much that I feel like I can contribute to that conversation, just because I've never had those experiences. So, um, they were having a conversation about school and the teachers and I, like, I don't know, the school, teachers, um, classroom settings, people being like "Oh, can I touch your hair"—things like that. Right? And it was very casual and I was—maybe I felt more at ease because I didn't, have to, like I didn't say anything regarding it. But it was very casual and I didn't feel panicky, I was just listening to that, to their experiences and I didn't feel anxious to talk to them.

There are several considerations here. First, that Maria referenced this conversation two more times demonstrates how uncommon such experiences can be. This is not surprising; in a society where we are meant to be beyond race, noticing or talking about race is itself racist (Bonilla-Silva, 2014). Second, to consider Heidi's story alongside Maria's reveals a bind: young White people simultaneously *must* and *cannot* engage in race talk with people of color. This ambivalence is informed, in part, by the linking of people of color with race. This bind is better understood alongside Maria's feelings about the encounter.

Finally, Maria shared that because she didn't feel called on to participate in the race talk, she "felt more at ease" and "didn't feel panicky." Her participation was liminal; she both "didn't say anything" and "didn't feel anxious to talk to them." I believe she felt comfortable listening to her Black friends share stories of the racism they encountered because she was not called to witness *as a White person*. In those moments, the Blackness of her friends' experiences was salient while her Whiteness was not, at least not within the conversation. The liminality of her experience permitted her to listen as an unraced *individual* to systemically oriented race talk. Maria seemed grateful to have been allowed to listen. Her gratitude could, unbeknownst to her, extend to her feeling exonerated; because she was not hailed as White, she did not feel implicated. She could listen and walk away. There is both possibility and risk in this. Her ability to listen without feeling panicky could permit her to access her Whiteness in vulnerable and productive ways. Yet it could also, as it seems to do here, allow her to consume their experiences, feel bad about them without reflecting on her own Whiteness. I explore witnessing, empathy, and antiracism further in Chapter 6.

*   *   *

So long as Whiteness is unmarked and normed within neoliberal ideologies of individualism, race is, for White people, largely the purview of the racial Other, as in anyone who doesn't identify as White (Fine, 1997). Their Whiteness seemed to prevent their entry into conversations about race with people of color, both because White people could imagine themselves as unraced, and because they had no way to participate without discomfort. Participants maintained an unsteady grasp on systemic antiracism. They recognized elements of racist structures and their complicity within those structures, but these recognitions were often cut short by neoliberal ideologies such as individualism.

Moreover, I believe the hyper-individualism of neoliberalism limited participants' imagination when it came to the collective impact of an individual's action. Neoliberal historical tellings individuate movements to people who become larger-than-life heroes, such as Nelson Mandela, Martin Luther King, and Rosa Parks, while obscuring the complex social movements undergirding these figures. Young people encounter these figures removed from the many who worked alongside them and provided them with material and spiritual support as they fought fierce resistance from the power they challenged (resistance that is too often conveniently removed from the historical record). Without context, young people have little with which to identify, and as a consequence have limited access to antiracist identities. Social action, including antiracism, becomes heroic and unimaginable.

Participants, including David, Jenny, Ben, Maria, and Ali, argued that the linkage between race as a topic and people of color had been forged in their race talk experiences, both official and unofficial, wherein all race talk centered around the lives or experiences of people of color. Because Whiteness requires the abdication of ethnicity (and by proxy, race) to people of color, as taken up in Chapter 2, White people imagine they are raceless, and so cannot fully participate in race talk, especially with people of color. Further, because WPP positions Whiteness as guilty individuals in need of absolution, there is no legitimate space for Whiteness within race talk other than personal apology, which, like in Maria's situation, is often inappropriate.

Therefore, individualism can cause White people to feel out of place in conversations about race. Ryan put it this way: "I think race, like when we talk about race, it's always about a minority. I think if you're White, like you're just White, but like when you talk about race it's always African Americans and Indian Americans, whereas you don't hear about Italian Americans." In our final group meeting, Jenny identified a depressive effect of this perspective: "Because we rely on other races to make our identity, so it's like when we're asked to think of how our race would respond, we don't know." Recognizing the ways Whiteness is imagined as a void, a social nothing wherein White people can pretend they are normal individuals, Jenny identified how White conceptions of Whiteness position White people as racially unaffiliated, without a foothold or stake in conversations about race and racism. For me, antiracism as a White person is all about naming and unpacking Whiteness so that White people can find their foothold, though this also posed risks.

Several participants feared that should they gather as White people to talk about Whiteness, they would risk being seen as White supremacists rather than antiracists. For example, when I proposed they might start a Whiteness book club, Ben was uneasy: "Forming a White book club or the term *White book club* really to me doesn't sound good." Similarly, Ryan and David argued that White people would refuse to participate in such a group for fear of being misread as racists. Several participants feared that any White-oriented antiracist work would be equated with the White supremacist exclusion they wanted to work against.

When I asked how they talked about their participation, many confessed that they did not talk about it outside of limited casual conversation with their families; indeed, outside of my class and these conversations, none of the participants had ever encountered race talk about Whiteness. Here, again, participants were in a bind: to address racism they *must* talk about Whiteness; however, because of the social structures of race and Whiteness, they *could not* talk about Whiteness. As Ryan said in our initial interview, "It just, it feels like we [White people] shouldn't be here, like we should be talking about this, but we shouldn't, but we need to." So long as "race" is an embodied quality of only specifically raced individuals, White people will struggle (and potentially resist!) locating themselves within race talk in the productive ways necessary for antiracist change.

Together with the models of schooling explored in Chapter 3, individualism and the fraught relationship between Whiteness and race limit antiracist possibilities. White participants' understandings of racism included aspects of structural inequalities, yet articulable notions of race remained individualistic, so antiracism was limited to confession and personal interventions. Without potential and actionable antiracisms, and without clarity on what, precisely, constitutes racism, personal interventions, however well intentioned, contribute to the punishing and self-defeating discourse of calling out.

CALL-OUT CULTURE

While calling out generates public awareness in ways that can bol-
ster important social movements, notably the #MeToo movement,
which generated changes in the movie industry in 2017, the impact
of calling out is complex and controversial.[2] I believe it is possible to
root all anxiety about race talk, including referential language, colormuteness, and color celebrate, in the fear of being called out as racist.
Participants expressed more concern about being called out than in
working against racism itself. As Ken observed, "I think if you have
a few ethnic people[3] in your classroom, I get really scared to say any
views that I have because I might offend them." As Perry (2002)
noted, the fear of offending someone is as often a self-interested fear
of being perceived as racist as it is of hurting someone's feelings. These
anxieties were sometimes visible as awkward performances of nonracism, where participants conspicuously named their lack of racism by
celebrating diversity, as explored in the previous chapter. As noted
by Winans (2010) and as I take up in Chapter 6, the emotional function of White students' rhetorical positionings are too often read as
resistance and "can function as a site of engagement and possibility"
(p. 475).

Moreover, individualized antiracist work can only amount to individualized censure, as more complex conversations about social structures are foreclosed. It is an environment that, as David put it,

> creates this power structure in which the more you call out people, the
> higher up you are in that social structure. You have people desperately
> looking for anything that can be deemed as racist or offensive in any way,
> just to increase their social status; "Hey, look, I'm more woke than you. I
> call out more racism than you do."

In her initial interview, Jenny suggested a similar motivation: "It
could also be someone that's just trying to like hide their thoughts
in a way they are doing something and raising awareness where you
just don't know their intentions at all." In other words, calling out
can be born, at least in part, out of self-preservation, or as an attempt
to secure an antiracist identity (Lensmire, 2017). Further, in an environment where being *called* racist is the worst, and possibly only,
committable racist sin, race talk itself becomes the embattled space,
so that calling out constitutes antiracism to the exclusion of broader
personal responsibility and social action. As David said, "You just

wait for some person to say the wrong thing and then it's a free-for-all." Here again, available models of racism leave young White people with little rhetorical footing and few actionable antiracist options.

As with other aspects of race talk, participants were somewhat aware of the shortcomings of the discourses available to them. In meeting 4, Ben questioned his own tendency to judge White classmates who argue that White people can experience racism. In doing so he inadvertently provided an example of how gleefully savage calling out can be:

> *Ben:* Yeah, um, so when people say that to me, my gut reaction is
>   like, "What a fucking idiot."
>   [loud laughter, nods, crosstalk]
> *Maria, others:* I was thinking the exact same thing!
> *Kevin/Ben:* [crosstalk] Okay—let's not, it's common . . .
> *Ben:* I do not, I do not let that thought stay in my head. Because
>   that's just, that's an awful thing to say about a classmate.
>   [laughter continues, Maria leans back eyes closed, Heidi leans
>   forward, both laughing hard]
> *Ben:* I do not let myself sustain that sense because that's very
>   toxic and it's not good.
> *Kevin:* [to Heidi] And you said something interesting; you, I think
>   you said, "I think he's a good person."
> *Heidi:* Yes, [small laugh]
> *Kevin:* And it seemed like him saying . . .
> *Heidi:* [covers her mouth laughing] That sounded bad now that
>   you say that.

Here, in our conversation about race talk with other White classmates, Ben shared his struggle to remain open-minded to those who disagree with him in certain ways, in this case those who believe White people can experience racism. Several other participants leapt on this as a sanctioned opportunity to position themselves as "better than" those less-woke White people by laughing and joking. While I experienced the same rush of recognition, he and I both attempted to challenge this response. I was reminded of a similarly toned comment Heidi had made as part of her attempt to reconcile a White classmate's racist views. Raising it in this context highlighted to Heidi what seemed to be her sense of moral superiority over a classmate, which, when examined, became distasteful.

However, Heidi also believed the corrections were her moral re-sponsibility. In her final interview, I asked Heidi what it might be like if she chose to not correct someone:

> I'd probably feel mad at myself because that person is going to continue in this world, and not like me saying this one thing is going to change their view, but it's gonna make me feel bad because this person is going to continue in the world, with what I think is not the whole picture [laughs] or I'll feel like I've done an injustice for myself, but also for that other person, because that person is not hearing the other side of that.

I don't know what to make of her altruistic motivation, what she means by "the whole picture." While it's certainly possible that she has en-gaged with someone genuinely ignorant of the other side she offered, I've very rarely, if ever, encountered a high school student without some history of the dichotomous perspectives available in these con-versations. Either way, while participants articulated understandings of the structural, historical, and contextual nature of racism, their per-formed understandings of race often fell into the same individualized construct embraced by WPP.

Other participants, even those who called out others, recognized the dangers of calling out. Ben and Ali both struggled to reconcile their desire to correct people with the risks of those corrections. Ali suggested those corrections should happen "not in a way that almost attacks them for thinking the way . . . but then again we do need to go deeper but, like a gentle approach." Ben shared that he would correct someone only if he could do so without being "an ass about it." While David most vocally cri-tiqued call-out culture, most participants expressed concern, frustration, or both, with call-out culture. Indeed, calling out seemed to be at the nexus of participants' understandings of, and anxieties about, race talk.

Once again, these moments of anxiety present us with an opportunity to pause, to breathe, and to check in with our bodies. Whiteness is at work in these moments to hurry us along, to obscure the underlying anxieties and thereby obscure the systems of power with which we are in tension. Because calling out is often a defensive distortion of antiracism, a projec-tion of White insecurities, the pathway to a more generative antiracism is through that defensiveness. In that way, by examining and processing the White racial anxiety and insecurity submerged in the body, Whiteness and not an individual White person becomes the object of critique.

*   *   *

Rather than addressing race talk as one part of systemic racism, calling out can be limited to discursive exchanges among White people. Locating racism within individuals serves to circumscribe race talk. The antiracist goal of engaging in race talk, then, becomes to censure race talk, effectively depressing conversation about race. Ali described the fear of being called out like this: "You don't want to say the wrong thing. So it's, I've never been corrected because I've never gone into detail with it. I've never had a very deep conversation about it with someone else." According to Linder (2015), this fear leads to "inauthentic relationships with people of Color, a distinct barrier to engaging in antiracist behavior" (p. 545). Indeed, several participants described being privy to but not a part of the race talk of their peers of color. Only David described having friendships with Black peers.

Lensmire (2017) found similar dynamics among White people, where "the threat of being labeled a racist stifled not just racist talk, but other talk that might not be racist but could be labeled that way" (p. 35). For his White interviewee, his had the effect of pushing all race talk underground to a "basement subculture" where, around a poker table, White people could be celebrated for pushing back against PC culture. In my initial interview with him, Ken shared a story that mirrored that almost exactly. Ken described how his group of mostly White male friends would, periodically, share jokes, attempting to find increasingly offensive jokes on a range of topics, including race:

Ken: I know that I don't think a lot of people do this and it doesn't happen all the time, but every now and then it's like you get this refresher, you know? Like every month or so we just spend like 30 minutes doing this, you know? Looking online at jokes.

Kevin: Interesting. And you say a refresher? What does that mean?

Ken: Well, I feel like it happens and then you get old of it pretty fast. Like you've heard all these jokes before.

Kevin: The fun kind of runs out.

Ken: The fun kind of runs out. So yeah, I think it also, the racism gets to you over time. I feel as though that happens. Like you start thinking about it.

Kevin: So it's kind of like you share jokes for a while and after a while, it's both like there aren't any more and, like, "I feel kind of too dirty to keep going," and then it sort of leaves the conversation for a month or something.

Ken: You start talking about something else, nobody speaks of it.

Like the basement subculture Lensmire (2017) explored, these sessions followed particular rules. While the rules seemed designed to keep the peace among participants, they also importantly remind us that these are performances of Whiteness doing specific work. In addition to responding to call-out culture, these could serve as Whitening rituals for Ken and his friends. As Ken described, "You want to make somebody laugh around you or you like, some people want to see people hurt and it's, it's all based on like either building or pushing away somebody. Like, building relationships in a way that, like, they find you funny." Lensmire (2017) explained it this way: "For me, Frank was pointing to the potential for any talk about race to be used in a struggle, *among white people*, over who is and who is not considered a 'good' white person" (p. 40, emphasis in original). In this way in/out groupings (explored in the next section) within Whiteness cut multiple ways.

Because calling out can simultaneously contribute to and inhibit antiracist efforts, addressing calling out is both complicated and necessary. For example, helpful critiques of calling out must not be assumed to be critiques of antiracism. David, who took up antiracist beliefs, was attuned to and frustrated by what he described as "virtuous" White behavior:

> I think it's like people—like you have White people who try, who try to appear more virtuous by not letting others talk about race. . . . They get to feel like they're the protector of, you know, Black people or something. But really it's just doing harm.

In addition to David, Joel spoke strongly against call-out culture. In our first and only conversation, I asked him who did the calling out in his experience. "There's a group that seems to be mostly White girls who are willing to be outspoken about these topics and will jump on anyone who comes near to them." Joel described this group as people who have "taken humanitarian efforts to heart," a phrase seemingly devised to soften his pejorative view of the group he saw so negatively.

While these criticisms could suggest comparable underlying attitudes toward racism, like the contrast between David's and Joel's concern about noticing racial disparities in academic contexts noted in Chapter 3, David's concern seems to align with the stated antiracism objectives of calling out, while Joel's seems to stem from his negative view of the political aim of calling out. These two more conservative participants, who have both experienced being called out, demonstrate how problematic calling out can be. Superficially, both David and Joel could each appear resistant to antiracism in the eyes of their peers or a high school teacher, yet David embraces antiracist ideas while Joel rejects them. Despite this difference, each could be read as resistant within the binary of call-out culture.

To more effectively facilitate race talk, we as classroom teachers would benefit from stepping away from the individualized call-out environment and instead provide more space to views superficially at odds with our understanding of antiracism. We must resist the temptation to take young White people's criticisms of what we believe is antiracism as shorthand for their more deeply held beliefs about race. We can at least name this problematic dynamic for our students. Further, like my self-interested critique of other less-woke White people, we risk enforcing the neoliberal individualized understanding of racism if our calling out is not accompanied by self-implication and systemic reflection.

Like much of antiracist action, call-out culture cannot be an end unto itself. Calling out has been credited for building awareness and action on issues such as sexual assault on college campuses (Vemuri, 2018). Other thinkers remain critical. "It isn't an exaggeration to say that there is a mild totalitarian undercurrent not just in call-out culture but also in how progressive communities police and define the boundaries of who's *in* and who's *out*" (Ahmad, 2015, p. 2, emphasis in original). A "forever shifting" set of language and terminology police these boundaries in highly public arenas like classrooms or, more commonly now, social media. These boundaries perpetuate a facile and, as Ben would say, reductionist, antiracism, while functioning to uphold White supremacy in historical ways, as I explore later. Besides, who feels inspired to self-reflect when being publicly shamed? Ultimately, as Jamie Utt (2015) wrote, "We must take up the long, difficult, often emotionally-exhausting work of calling them in to change" (para. 12).

The more I have been able to remain mindful of the workings of Whiteness and White supremacy and the deep woundedness White folks have experienced, the more I have gained perspective for the missteps and racist views of other White people. Moreover, I find that as I attend to my own woundedness, the indignation inherent to my calling out (rather than calling in) falls away. The more I engage in my own work, the more time I spend attendant to my own Whiteness in my body, the more grounded I am in those sometimes tense interactions, and the more I can avoid grouping White people as in or out.

IN/OUT GROUPINGS WITHIN WHITENESS

In/out boundaries of White progressivism were evident among participants. Within our conversations, so far as I could tell, only David and Ken were censured by the other participants, though Joel would likely have been censured as well had he participated in the meetings. For Ken, following his description of an experience with people of color in a group meeting, the video recording showed Jenny glancing at me, while Heidi exchanged glances with Ali, in what I interpreted as a moment where they believed Ken had potentially crossed a discursive line. For David, the censure was verbal. As he shared his skepticism on an example of cultural appropriation, Heidi raised her hand and disagreed, the only such exchange in our conversations. These moments contrast with an exchange early in meeting 4. For a senior project, Ben was investigating referential language, and in checking in with the group, he asked why people chose the descriptor *African American* over *Black* or *Negro*. There was a 3-second pause wherein no one batted an eye before Ben clarified that no one uses *Negro* anymore, whereupon we all released the tension with loud laughter and jokes. We then cheerfully moved on. Had Ken or David stated this, I'm confident the reaction would have been different.

Participants' willingness to entertain Ben's use of the word *Negro*, even for those few seconds, demonstrated that he was *in*, that other participants recognized his position as a potential authority on what may or may not constitute racism. In the absence of people of color, Ben was positioned as a racial expert, so that if he used the word *Negro*, his use was assumed to be justified and beyond censure. Meanwhile, David and Ken, censured by other participants, were *out*, at least more out than the other participants. More broadly, all participants seemed to understand an "in/out" divide among their peers, between those who took up the liberal perspective that racism was a problem requiring antiracist work and those who, for whatever reason, (or seemingly in whatever way), disagreed. In a clear expression of a bind, David told me that the only productive conversations about race involved those who were "out," in that those were the White people needing to learn more and be converted. However, only those who were "in," who already appreciated systemic racial issues, would attend such conversations so that they would be preaching to the choir, so to speak.

As I noted earlier, despite my attempts to recruit White participants with a range of views on race, the nine participants who constituted the bulk of the work all viewed racism as a serious problem worthy of their attention and effort. Despite this alignment, or perhaps as a result of it, there was a fissure based not on who embraced antiracism and who did not (as would have been the case had Joel participated), but one seemingly based on the relative wokeness of the participants (as David suggested there would be). David, Ken, and Ryan had all expressed more conservative views beforehand and would likely have been recognizable as such to other participants. Indeed, Ben mentioned to me later that he was surprised at Ryan's more liberal perspective. Their responses were therefore surveilled differently; even though they shared the goal of fighting racism, their views were inherently suspicious because of their being "out."

Finally, despite being censured by other participants as being "out," David's embrace of antiracism was as cogent as any participant's. Indeed, it's possible he was censured *because of* his insight; his legitimate criticisms of calling out as counterproductive could have been read as resistance to antiracism, and therefore deserving of censure. "Policing the boundaries of who's *in* and who's *out*" embraces close-mindedness where new ways of thinking are required (Ahmad, 2015, p. 2, emphasis in original). It also has a long history within White supremacy.

*　　*　　*

This practice of carefully policed boundaries within a group of White people echoes early processes of Whitening itself, where Whiteness in the 18th and early 19th centuries was treated like a resource to be held as property and protected, as described in Chapter 2. The power of Whiteness has always been rooted in and wielded through its contestability and opacity. By requiring that Irish immigrants take up wage labor, racism, and nativism to gain access to Whiteness, White elites enfranchised the Irish at the expense of their ethnic identities and class solidarity, to the benefit of the elites. In this way, White supremacy maintained itself by redirecting Irish anti-American sentiment away from those in power and toward those less powerful than them, namely Black laborers (Roediger, 1991).

As racism shifted from a de jure to de facto role in society and multiculturalism and colorblindness, which served to submerge racist structures of power that became "official antiracisms" after WWII, racism became located in the less educated, so that a person's capacity to *declare* their antiracism served as their token of good White nonracism (Melamed, 2011). Here, rather than legally disenfranchising those who fall outside of Whiteness in de facto White supremacy, those who are "out," become culturally and economically disenfranchised, as written about extensively in the wake of the 2016 presidential election.[4] Nonetheless, the mechanism of White supremacy is the same. The artificial partitioning of good Whiteness and Whiteness's complementary loathsomeness, along with the capricious boundaries of call-out culture, mimic the earlier divide of White from Black, and each serve to direct negative energy away from power holders.

In keeping with the view that racism does not "get better" on its own, but rather adapts to the social norms of the day, Whiteness no longer needs to explicitly alienate people of color. Rather, White supremacy can be maintained, in part, through uncritical call-out culture, a Whiteness through wokeness, where antiracist action feebly stalls through anxious White performances. Within a social context where race talk happens, members of the group will, over time, come to understand their position in a hierarchy of racial awareness, in part because of the public nature of calling out. That race talk itself, in its contestability, volatility, and intensity, can determine the social and moral status of White people among their White peers deserves closer attention.

As pedagogues we must be cautious that our antiracist work does not, as White privilege pedagogy has, contribute to this binary. By constructing a conceptual binary based on verbal and public confession, WPP divides students into two groups, those "good" White people who have confessed to their privilege and the "bad" White people who have not. The goal, then, within this project is to exact a public confession, rescuing resistant "bad" students by transforming them into "good" students who confess (Lensmire et al., 2013; Levine-Rasky, 2000). Conceived as a classroom operation, WPP depends on this fatuous in/out divide among White students, where teachers determined to impart the severity of racism (as a demonstration of their *own* White goodness) cajole "bad" students to convert, and might even enlist "good" White students to convince their reluctant classmates.

As a novice pedagogue working against racism, I embraced this divide, however uneasily, feeling both bound to it as an available antiracist practice and convinced that there must be better options. The inevitable result was a classroom speciously arranged according to how seriously young White people took up confession, with those confessors who were "in" most emphatically on one side, and the rest, positioned as socially and morally inferior, on the other. As teacher, I oscillated between addressing myself to the "bad" White students in hopes of "correcting" them, and attempting to facilitate dialogue between the "good" and "bad" White students, so that the "good" ones might, through logic or shame, convince the "bad" students to embrace confession.

I also cannot deny a seductive insularity I experienced in these conversations. I felt somewhat justified prioritizing my antiracist efforts ahead of students' well-being, as though the shame felt by resistant students was itself evidence of antiracist work. Solely by nature of facilitating those conversations, I was beyond reproach. I was "in." My classroom was an arena wherein I could be unchallenged, confusing, as Freire (2007) said, the authority of knowledge with my personal authority. More insidiously, working within this binary felt clear and definitive. It felt *good*. This clarity now causes me to pause. White moral superiority, I believe, lies close to White supremacy, wherein my moral outrage became centered, and, like in confession and calling out, recentered my Whiteness in dangerous and narcissistic ways. When Whiteness is not centered in the name of decentering it, antiracism isn't served; White supremacy is.

Rather, as Loretta Ross (2019) wrote in a recent *New York Times* op-ed titled "I'm a Black Feminist. I Think Call-Out Culture Is Toxic," we can embrace calling in:

> We can change this culture. Calling-in is simply a call-out done with love. Some corrections can be made privately. Others will necessarily be public, but done with respect. It is not tone policing, protecting white fragility or covering up abuse. It helps avoid the weaponization of suffering that prevents constructive healing. (para. 18)

This is countercultural and will take time and effort to resist the toxicity of calling out. But moving against White supremacy with love rather than anxiety can help shift the conversation beyond White self-reflection.

GOOD WHITE NONRACISM, BAD WHITE ANTIRACISM?

Individualism, calling out, and in/out groupings within Whiteness each affect participants' conceptions of antiracism, as noted. There are several additional ways of thinking that seemed to get in the way of participants' imagined antiracisms. In this section I explore how different participants discuss antiracist possibilities, in particular how participants' political ideologies seemed to inform their sense of what seemed possible.

To begin, Jenny explained feeling caught between the belief that she could take up antiracism and a worldview that positioned her as powerless:

> *Jenny:* It's kind of like, I don't know, I feel like because I don't know what to do, it's kind of like degrading or like, [I] kind of feel like, like I feel like there's not much I can do but there is.
>
> *Kevin:* There isn't much, but there is.
>
> *Jenny:* Yeah. [laughs]
>
> *Kevin:* Yeah, what's that about?
>
> *Jenny:* I feel like being like or not like I'm not a politician or whatever, like there's not much I can do, but there is, like it's not—and I hope like other people feel like they can do something. I don't know. It's kind of a weird feeling.
>
> *Kevin:* Yeah. Yeah.
>
> *Jenny:* Cause it's like, I don't know, you feel like guilty for not doing anything but you want to do something.

Jenny, like the other participants, recognized her implication in Whiteness and racism, meaning that "not being a politician" was not an adequate response to racism. Further, I believe her use of "degrading" gets at the emotional toll of remaining responsible without feeling empowered. Ali made a similar comment about antiracism in her final interview:

> Um, sometimes I feel like I should know that I should do something. I don't even know. I just, I feel like there's something right in front of me that I know I should do, but I don't know what that is.

She shared this despondently, as though her own personal goodness was also just out of reach in front of her. Both examples could more hopefully suggest that these young White people are still learning about race, and that with time they will come to a better understanding of how White supremacy can be resisted. Indeed, this is how I read their situation. Yet they do not express optimism here about developing an antiracist identity, nor do they suggest that they have more to learn.

In contrast, while Ryan struggled in similar ways, he did not seem nearly as affected by feeling caught. In fact, as we explored this bind he began laughing:

> *Kevin:* You're laughing a little bit. What do . . .
> *Ryan:* I don't know. This—when we talked this was the one I
>   had the most difficulty with. It's just hard to think of specific
>   ideas 'cause, you can be, not racist, but it's basically like
>   going out, and as a White person trying to be antiracist is, it's
>   like a whole different thing, I feel like. . . . I think it's very
>   easy to not say the n-word, all these things, and then just
>   carry on with your life. And I think to me it's very difficult
>   to go one step further.

Ryan seemed struck by how "one step further" actually represented an ideological shift, "a whole different thing" as he put it, between not being racist and being antiracist. I interpret his laughter as responding to both the absurd failure of his schooling on race and how daunting antiracism, when it begins to come into view, actually is. Similarly, David shared clear insights about his and his peers' struggles with antiracism and struggled to identify antiracist actions he might take up. Yet he, like Ryan, seemed able to name and accept the broader context of this bind:

> I think a lot, you know, like you say racism and it's like this, you know,
> big evil word up in the clouds. If everyone says, you know, "I'm not rac-
> ist, it's other people who are doing this." Like it's hard to, 'cause, like it's
> not like I could go through my day, like as a White person, do all the stuff
> I normally do and then just every so often point out "that's an oppres-
> sive thing, that's an oppressive thing. You shouldn't do that." . . . Like
> what's something small that you could do? And I'm just like, I have no
> idea. Like what's something small as I think that's, I think that's kind of
> because like White, like if you're in the culture of Whiteness you kind
> of have this protected aura where like you don't really ever need to like
> change anything. So when the time comes where it's like okay think of
> something you can change, you got nothing.

While each participant struggled to name what they could do to address racism, I was struck by the differences between partici-pants who seemed "in," like Jenny and Ali, and those who seemed "out," including David and Ryan. While David and Ryan seemed equally bewildered by antiracism, they did not seem to take that bewilderment *personally* the way Jenny and Ali did. It is possible to read David and Ryan's relative comfort with their struggle as disinterest, or emotional distance; that Jenny and Ali identified as more liberal, and as women, could also suggest this. However, the uneven ways participants seemed comfortable taking up Whiteness complicates this.

Moreover, the more conservative participants, including Ken, Ryan, and David, were all more comfortable exploring Whiteness as deficit as well as an antiracist possibility. In our sixth group meeting, I asked participants to share, as I put it, "what's hard about being White or, or what being, like, what is lost, or missing as a, as a White person?" David began by raising the negative impact of the American melting pot on White people:

> I feel like if you, you know, become White, it's kind of like the whole, you're thrown into the melting pot kind of thing. You know, like, uh, sure someone can be like, you know, German or Irish, all, you know, different kinds like that. But I feel like, if you're White, you're just lumped into the overarching group of White people and whatever nationality you had is lost.

Ryan continued:

> I think there's something about culture being gained when you're in the minority or oppressed group. It's kind of like, we need our culture to rise up. I think White people just don't really need that. They don't need the culture to rise up, to like, band as one. So I think that kind of impacts that.

I want to note that this view risks an over-identification explored in Chapter 6; we are cautioned by Minnie Bruce Pratt:

> I was using Black people to weep for me, *to express my sorrow at my responsibility, and that of my people, for their oppression*: and I was mourning because I felt they had something I didn't, a closeness, a hope, that I and my folks had lost because we tried to shut other people out of our hearts and lives. (as quoted in Boler, 1999, p. 165, emphasis in original)

Finally, Ken added, "I mean like David, Ryan both said, I think you lose a lot of culture when you become White, and a little bit of your personality too; there's certain stereotypes of which race you are."

These views could reflect the historical perspectives of the development of Whiteness, including Thandeka's (2001) work with Whiteness as loss. Additionally, they lend themselves to Logue's (2005) argument that White privilege should be counter-read as perilous as well as beneficial. In other words, teaching Whiteness to young people as, at best, a mixed bag, might make it a little easier for those people to critically examine their Whiteness. A new, complicated telling would also counter the shamed-based better than/worse than understanding of racial identity, which, at this point, informs everything from White ethno-nationalism to White shame and guilt. I explore new ways of making sense of racial identity in Chapter 6.

These sympathetic views of people struggling with their Whiteness were not taken up by the group's more liberal members. Ben, while not disagreeing, complicated these deficit views: "If I propose like thinking of Whiteness as a loss rather than a privilege, if I propose that to someone who is not White, I would, in effect, step on a mine." Ali agreed. I share this caution, and I believe it is well placed. Even these comments raise significant concerns, as noted. However, we are reminded that there is no perfect antiracism (Kumashiro, 2002) and that taking up Whiteness critically *does* allow for antiracist possibilities (Jupp & Slattery, 2010). Perhaps more importantly, antiracism as a White person is about reclaiming wholeness and authenticity. There are no single paths toward healing, and so long as we take care to not reify Whiteness, the more possibilities available the better. Our work benefits from potential ways of being; if we can't imagine what we are working toward, we can only act against what we want to work away from, and "acting against" is a working of Whiteness. We need new ways of knowing, thinking, acting, and being. As Audre Lord reminds us, we will never dismantle the master's house with the master's tools.

As a final example, I invited participants to share something tangible they could do to address racism in our final group meeting. Several participants shared self-improvement possibilities, including reading; "train yourself to push back on negative stereotypes regarding other races" (David); "write down your thoughts" (Jenny); and "just talking about racism and letting yourself be wrong. Just going into it with the idea that you have something to learn" (Ben). As a caution, participants' expressed understandings of potential antiracisms in no way commit them to action. For young White people, learning more about Whiteness, race, and racism are legitimate and meaningful steps they can take to develop their "race cognizance" (Frankenberg,

1993). Yet, like White privilege confessionals, these can serve as a safe stopping point well before participants take steps to make change.

Despite Whiteness being a central focus of our conversations, Ken was the only participant to suggest that exploring his White ancestry could be an antiracist act:

> I would say looking at your past, like your family's past and stuff. They won't always generally go positively for you but if you know who you are and how different you are and stuff, it can make you sensitized to other cultures and other people's past. It could also go the other way.

Ken's willingness to embrace Whiteness as a potentially antiracist topic contrasts with the more liberal participants, whose reluctance stemmed from their fear that they might be censured for proposing, as Ben put it, that "Whiteness is a loss rather than a privilege." Yet Ken did not, and nor do I, propose that Whiteness's losses offset its privileges, or that they could not exist side by side, and Ken cautioned against the potential for White ethno-nationalism.

That examining Whiteness as a deficit was so distasteful to participants who expressed a sincere desire for antiracist possibilities is striking. Like the more liberal participants' fatalism about antiracism, there seemed to be little ambiguity in this rejection. Insofar as more conservative participants explored this, they were ignored or cautioned by the rest of the group. I wondered how other liberal discourses of Whiteness negatively affect participants' senses of antiracist possibilities. All participants were similarly bound by available discourses, including the need to recognize the severity of racism alongside White moral responsibility, explored earlier. Yet the more liberal participants seemed more deeply mired in this bind. What if aspects of good Whiteness, including feeling bad about racism, get in the way of antiracism?

I emphasize again that White people taking up Whiteness in the pursuit of antiracism *is* fraught and can prove detrimental. And this could be a moment to, as Trainor (2002) suggests, "embrace discourses that we might have once preferred not to honor, even with our gaze" (p. 648), *within the context* of conversations about race among White people. Zembylas (2012) clarifies, "The focus is to use strategic naivety and empathy to draw out students who hold what we might consider uncritically hegemonic positions—to provide a connection with, however temporarily, to 'views that one may find unacceptable or offensive'" (p. 120). I explore this further in Chapter 6.

Is it possible that more liberal White participants are beholden to the approval of their liberal White peers in ways that prevent antiracist possibilities? Do they so fear taking up antiracism in ways that might be perceived as insincere or ill-intentioned that they struggle to take it up at all? Perhaps there is a point at which the worse young White people believe racism to be, the more they see it as this "big evil word up in the clouds," as David said, the less capable they feel to do something about it.

In his review of the history of race and racism in the United States, Kendi (2016) noted three stances taken up in response to racism: segregationist, assimilationist, and antiracist. Following this, I explored good White people's responses to racism in terms of nonracism and antiracism, where nonracism can be understood as neoliberal multiculturalism, such as learning more about people of color, rather than exploring and dismantling systems of racial oppression. This follows Leonardo and Zembylas (2013) where,

> "non-racist" becomes an identity, even a badge of honor, whereas antiracism is arguably a political pledge, a form of race labor, to combat racism before it ossifies into an identity. To the non-racist, it is something one is; to the anti-racist, it is something one does. (p. 156)

Most participants' response to racism, especially the more conservative members, fit the description of a nonracist. However, despite anxieties about discussing Whiteness, these more conservative participants were also more comfortable than liberal participants with taking up Whiteness in the pursuit of antiracism. The more liberal participants resisted this possibility and expressed stark ambivalences about antiracism, which seemed simultaneously accessible and hopelessly out of reach to them. They were left feeling pessimistic or apathetic about antiracism, which is more than enough to derail White antiracist possibilities.

It is not surprising that other well-intentioned White people feel similarly bound and express similar anxieties. In their study of how colorblindness is taken up by White rural teachers, Lee-Nichols and Tierney (2018) noted how, "by fearing that they might get things wrong and harm the students of color in their classrooms, these White teachers are always already made as confused, uncertain, or, worst of all, racist by the discourses available for talking about race in their communities" (p. 57). These young White people seemed similarly "always already" positioned within challenging or impossible discourses of race talk, even among their White peers. Participants seemed governed by the gap between the available discourses of neoliberal individualism and the systemic nature of race and White supremacy, and hindered by the anxious antiracist performances of their White peers. Without the language of systemic racism with which to name their feelings and experiences of race and racism, White people are left with inadequate and sometimes inappropriate languages and ideologies of individualized actions and repercussions.

CONCLUSION

The bulk of this project (and my own antiracist work) has become working toward clearing a path to new ways of being,[5] rather than accumulating new histories or theories or just about anything that can be found in a book. The work for me has been about building ways of knowing based on rereading history and processing theories, but all in service to getting out of my own way. In other words, I'm held back not by a lack of knowledge or the newest analysis, but by my ongoing investments in White ways of being and ways of seeing the world. Antiracist work, I am coming to understand, is heart and body work. My mind must be addressed so that it can get out of my way, and I believe the following chapter identifies some of those obstacles, but the real work of social change begins internally, as we have known all along. The rest of this book will focus on emotion and working toward new ways of being and feeling in the world.

So long as racism is taken up within a hyper-individualized neoliberal context, prejudices, including racism, are divorced from the social structures that perpetuate them. These structures would serve as a ballast to the isolating personal struggle with race. By recognizing the social context wherein White individuals might gain perspective on their internalized White supremacy, they might be better able to work against it. Without these contexts, young White people are left to reckon with racism individually. Unable to locate the origin of their racist thoughts outside of themselves, they are likely to consider themselves as the origin of these unwelcome thoughts, miring them in guilt and shame. As Althusser explains, through interpellation, "persons choose to identify with the ideologies that 'summon' them; in turn they understand themselves to be the source, rather than the effect of that summons" (as quoted in Britzman, 1991, p. 223). Individualism not only decontextualizes the experiences of people of color, it sequesters

White people from potentially helpful collective understandings of their internalized White supremacy, along with the potential for collective healing. In other words, White privilege pedagogy has undervalued the impact of emotion and troubled knowledge, especially among members of the oppressor group, in ways that have, at a minimum, alienated White people from anti-oppressive possibilities.

CHAPTER 5

Antiracism and Emotionality

So, when people talk about all this crap that's gone down and like with the Civil War, I'm kind of wondering what the hell do you expect me to feel or do about it. Like yeah it was tragic but that was 150 years ago, and my family wasn't even here. So you can't even guilt me into the old White plantation thing. It's like I literally had nothing to do with this and you're gonna blame me because of my skin color and expect me to feel bad about it.

—Joel (personal interview, January 18, 2019)

Joel was the group's erstwhile 10th participant. While he expressed interest in fully participating and never withdrew or declined, he and I only conducted an initial interview. In spite of his absence, he was a central figure in my work. His absence afforded new perspectives on in/out groupings and stucknesses within liberal Whiteness, and our conversation shaped the focus of my work on emotion. Specifically, I want to take seriously Joel's question, "What do you expect me to feel about it?" I believe the question is important; teachers, myself included, have not seemed to have clear outcomes in mind when addressing racism. For myself, I wanted my learners to appreciate the horrors of historical racism and to recognize the contemporary manifestations of those horrors, often by reading and watching accounts of Black bodies subjected to violence. To answer Joel's question simply, I wanted them to feel *bad* about it. Yet I also needed them to feel bad about it in recognizable ways, so that I would *know* that they felt bad. That way I could determine the success of my pedagogy. So perhaps what I wanted was for them to *seem like* they felt bad about it. In a way, the worse they seemed to feel, the more successful my pedagogy, and the better *I* was permitted to feel as an antiracist educator. In my classroom, like in many others, learners who failed to effectively perform in this way were considered resistant holdouts in need of convincing. They were resisting antiracism, and often subjected to calling out, as explored in Chapter 4. In this chapter I expand my analysis of the emotional

maneuvers taken up by White people. I try to make sense of participants' anger and deep uncertainty. I look to resources on empathy and
trauma to better access the sources underlying participants' emotions
related to race. Ultimately, I find significant shortcomings in the ways
resistance and shame are understood in the literature on Whiteness.

RESPONSES TO WPP

As Chubbuck and Zembylas (2008) argue, the purpose of attending to
emotion is so that "teachers and students from the dominant culture
begin to identify unconscious privileges as well as invisible ways in
which they comply with dominant ideology" (p. 286). Moreover, I
encountered emotion in every aspect of my work with these White
participants. In part because I worked hard to elicit an emotional response; the classroom atmosphere was highly charged, despite the
tightly controlled White faces in front of me. What was happening
inside of my students? Moreover, what was happening inside the students who took up my pedagogy and felt bad about racism? What did
it mean when White students who felt bad about racism continued to
encounter sanctioned and horrific violence year after year after year
with little if any emotional support?

Like critiques of WPP, which identify its failure to take up antiracism (Lensmire et al., 2013), Gardner (2017) is critical of exposing
young people to depictions of violent racism, "Now, so many years
later, I ask, 'What did our teachers expect us to gain from the exposure?'" (p. 338). For Gardner, the crisis happens with young Black
students. I believe the concern applies, broadly speaking and in different ways, to young White people encountering depictions of racial violence in the classroom, particularly when those exposures are
so poorly supported. Many of the participants described their early
encounters with race as vivid and uncomfortable memories of images or videos of racial violence. Deborah Britzman (2000) calls these
histories "difficult knowledge," which can be understood as "those
moments when knowledge appears disturbingly foreign or inconceiv-
able to the self, bringing oneself up against the limits of what one is
willing and capable of understanding" (Simon, as quoted in Zembylas,
2014, p. 392). Unsurprisingly, because of the sensitive and emotional
nature of the knowledge, effectively deploying difficult knowledges in
the context of high school classrooms presents significant challenges.
I take up these challenges in Chapter 6.

Insofar as we have used historical racisms to teach about race, I believe WPP can and has misapplied these knowledges. As reviewed in Chapter 2, WPP seeks to counter the assumption of racial equality inherent in neoliberal colorblindness. Unfortunately, WPP, itself an incomplete stand-in for critical pedagogy, is often deployed in clumsy ways by anxious White teachers (Chubbock & Zembylas, 2008). This pedagogy can take the form of subjecting students to violent or traumatic histories, often without emotional or even pedagogical support. Further, I believe these exposures can cause young White people to associate race talk with these exposures, hardening them against race talk out of self-preservation (to say nothing of aligning these exposures with race itself).

These exposures can look like unsupported encounters with depictions of racial violence, or they can look like Heidi's belief that scenes of violence on the Edmund Pettus Bridge were a necessary part of her antiracist education, that they "should talk about the brutalities of it too." I'm also reminded of Maria's guilt for not wanting to witness more violence inflicted upon civil rights protesters of the 1960s. Not only did participants share (and commiserate over!) troubling stories of these encounters, they seemed to believe that they were helpful or even necessary parts of their antiracist education.

By exploring how participants articulated their emotional experiences of race talk, I hope to better understand how guilt and shame interacted with their sense of themselves as antiracists. This examination must also consider how participants seemed positioned by the discourses available to them; namely, how WPP has influenced what participants believe they *ought* to feel. For this reason, I'm also curious about the role of performance within WPP.

I want to interject a quick note on language use. While guilt and shame are distinct emotional experiences, most participants seemed to use the terms interchangeably. Indeed, the phrase *white guilt* can suggest a state of being rather than remorse for a specific action ("I feel ashamed of my internalized racism" rather than "I feel guilty for laughing at a racist joke"). Further, "Silvan S. Tomkins—one of the background figures of contemporary affect theory—defines shame by first abandoning the traditional psychoanalytic distinction between shame and guilt. Instead, he proposes that both share a common currency, 'the affect of indignity, of defeat, of transgression, and of alienation'" (Schaefer, 2019, p. 5). I will follow that here.

Broadly speaking, there are two potential movements learners can make in response to WPP: they can take up the difficult knowledges of racism, which are most readily available to them through shame (I'm White, therefore I'm complicit and must confess to privilege), or they can reject them. These responses and their effects are explored next.

REJECTING WPP

Those who reject the premise of White privilege pedagogy are frequently read as resistant to the *object* of the pedagogy, antiracism, rather than the pedagogy itself. Before undertaking this work, I had understood this rejection as signaling a range of beliefs, including (I admit) self-centeredness, conservatism, and myopia, along with the rejection of antiracism. However, because this racial pedagogy has been focused on forcing a kind of crisis where young White people are asked to consider themselves as failures and perform shame, rejecting WPP can be a form of self-protection, in addition to upholding neoliberal post-racial attitudes. It can, as I explore next, signal generative resistance and critical thinking.

Joel, Ryan, and to a lesser degree David all rejected the premise of WPP. For Joel, there was no space in the antiracist pedagogy he had encountered to deal with historical racisms without a personal responsibility in the form of guilt or shame. His unwillingness, for whatever reason, to take up WPP seemed to extend to antiracism itself; that historical racisms inform contemporary inequalities was eclipsed by his rejection of the guilt being asked of him. Essentially, he rejected WPP's premise as well as its aim. To him, WPP is likely comparable to or indistinguishable from antiracism itself. Because he chose to not participate in our conversations, I was unable to explore this further with him. Yet the vitriol with which he rejected WPP speaks to an emotional underpinning, likely informed by repeated encounters with being called out by classmates and lectured by teachers. Joel's language indicates his anger at being told to feel guilty for historical racism, "You can't even guilt me into the old White plantation thing," and "You're gonna blame me because of my skin color and expect me to feel bad about it." It's not hard to imagine the teacher or classmate to whom he is responding, or how these conversations might push Joel to take up being "out" with a wounded pride (or even, in an extreme case, to explore the reactionary shelter of White nationalism).

Antoine Banks research on public policy debates such as health care or immigration showed how intense emotions like anger can become deeply intertwined with race as a topic. His work demonstrates the central role of emotion in White sense-making about race and affirms how Joel's feelings (like all of our feelings) can be primed by the idea of race itself, further foreclosing conversation. Conversely, Banks found that anger itself can trigger political belief systems about race for White people, so the feeling can *precede* political attitudes in addition to informing them. My personal experience with White men, whose anger about something incidental recalls for them a litany of historical and political wrongs, confirms this. That emotion and reason operate in tandem can feel commonsense, yet it runs counter to our deeply held belief in mind–body dualism, as explored in Chapter 2.

Thus, WPP itself can, over repeated exposures, pose a threat to young White people skeptical of WPP, as well as create increasingly charged conversations. Contributing to this, multiculturalism and some antiracist teachers like myself have weaponized the threat of being called racist as a way to impart the severity of racism. I have also, by not recognizing or challenging it, sustained the belief that internalized racism implies that one *is* racist. In other words, WPP has deployed the historical injustices of slavery or Jim Crow as a cudgel. I have relied on the internalized anxiety of White people to believe that I am doing a "good job" of teaching about race. Students who resist this, in addition to "needing convincing," might be taking refuge from an assault by being willing to reject the "goodness" of a confession of White privilege and the acceptance of White guilt that accompanies it. These resistant White students, like all of us, rely on models of goodness, though theirs lies outside of WPP. Antiracist work, unlike WPP, values actions and outcomes over ideologies. My work demonstrates the antiracist possibilities of young White people in part *because of* their resistance to WPP. Students like Joel are othered by some aspects of critical pedagogy (Trainor, 2002), and whatever classroom discourses are afforded by his exclusion must be weighed against that loss.

As explored in Chapter 3, Joel espoused views on race that some might find offensive and racist, including that there are biological explanations for the achievement gap in education. As far as these views represent the mainstream prejudices and racisms antiracists seek to address, Joel's rejection of WPP represents a significant failure to address them effectively. Despite not engaging in our conversations, Joel had agreed to participate and was forthcoming in his initial interview. Had there been space within the pedagogy he encountered, I believe his desire to learn and grow (shared by all of us) could have generated positive change. Our classroom work benefits from complicating our understandings of our students, especially those whose espoused beliefs are at odds with inclusive norms.

Ryan, on the other hand, rejected WPP without also rejecting antiracism by advocating for action without guilt:

> On the White guilt thing, I'm not, like I'm not waking up every morning saying "I feel bad for like, things in the past" because, I didn't, like, I didn't do that, it's not on my hands. So, don't, it's not me thinking "I feel bad for this." It's like when I see, would see an injustice or something, it's not like, because I'm White, this is an issue. It's . . . this is an issue because of things that happened in the past not tied to me? Does that make sense at all?

In my initial analysis Ryan's perspective seemed, as I wrote at the time, "dangerously close to colorblindness." I don't believe that holds. Rather, I think Ryan has positioned himself as a potential antiracist actor outside of WPP, which would call on him to take up guilt and shame for his Whiteness. This leaves him relatively unencumbered as he considers antiracism. Yet even as he positions himself as an antiracist actor, he seems uncertain at the end of his comment. I wonder if this meant that he sensed that by not feeling guilty for being White, he might be running afoul of the ethics of WPP.

Perhaps more importantly, resistance to official discourses (especially pedagogies) is exactly what's called for in critical pedagogy. This recalls Trainor's (2002) examination of how critical pedagogy problematically "others" those who resist it. As she points out, not only does this foster an us/them binary, it alienates resistance, the action at the heart of critical theory. I cannot afford to alienate students who resist my pedagogy when their resistance is the mechanism I hope to cultivate. Indeed, becoming an antiracist in a racist society is, in some ways, an ultimate expression of resistance. Yet, problematically, WPP suggests that successful antiracist teachers must convince resistant students of White privilege, leaving little or no room for resistance. While this is perhaps the largest failing of WPP, it is also how we can make sense of its popularity.

WPP focuses on developing White goodness in sanctioned ways, specifically through confession and supplication. By nature of introducing the model, White teachers become the primary White confessors without having to actually confess. When White teachers sanction the White privilege activity, we default to the "in" group and invite students to join us. This positions students as beholden to their more knowledgeable (and morally superior in wokeness) teachers. In contrast, the kind of empowered, outspoken, resistant antiracisms needed to overcome White supremacy are sometimes exactly the kind of disruptive resistance we often don't want to see in our classrooms. For my part, the White students who confessed to their privilege were, nearly to a person, "my people." They tended to say hello to me in the hallways, to ask after my day or my health, and gave my lessons the benefit of the doubt. I was grateful for their presence in my classroom and looked forward to a class where they constituted a majority of my students. In a word, they were easy to teach. Indeed, in the context of WPP, they were "done": they already accomplished the goal of the lesson. I faced the resistant students with what I considered a generous resolve. Convincing them was the difficult and sometimes painful work of antiracist education. Again, more difficult and more painful work in WPP indicated "real" antiracist work rather than a structural or conceptual failure. What other pedagogy would tolerate this?

My interview with Joel, quoted at the beginning of this chapter, is indicative of the resistance many of my students felt toward WPP. Yet the response to that resistance, the frustration and anger experienced by those who took up WPP, by me even in the context of that interview, is assumed and largely unexamined. I've shared that quote many times since to redirect that frustration and anger away from Joel and toward the flawed structure of WPP. Nearly every time the White people with whom I shared it shook their heads in the same frustrated and angry recognition I felt conducting the interview; I have been so conditioned by WPP that my frustration nearly overcame my practiced discipline as a researcher. Like participants who took up WPP, I had fundamentally misunderstood antiracism to be a debate between these two groups of White people.

TAKING UP WPP

The more liberal participants seemed almost eager to take up White privilege pedagogy, as explored in Chapter 3. However, taking up WPP rarely seemed to translate to even potential antiracist action. Those who took this up tended to do so in one of three ways, by taking up a multicultural empathy through literature and film, feeling caught, or both, as I explore in the following section. To a person, they all expressed helplessness in the face of racism.

I believe this helplessness stemmed from their pedagogy about racism, which has been focused on forcing a crisis where effects of shame and guilt, not antiracism, were signs of success. Students were to *feel* bad and *do* nothing. This is evident in Heidi's struggle to answer my question about what she can do to be antiracist during our final conversation,

> *Heidi:* Hmm, that's a hard question. So like, what's something like I could do?
> *Kevin:* Mhmm.
> *Heidi:* Or just like, what I—okay. Hmm. I think . . .
> *Kevin:* It can be hypothetical.
> *Heidi:* Yeah. Well I think . . . for me I think, definitely . . . like . . . I'm not, no, that's not how I want to word it. I think a place to start would be to, yeah, I guess recognize more like artwork or books or TV shows. Just things in my life that are around me that are by people of color.

Despite Heidi's demonstrated understanding of systemic racism, commitment to antiracism, and her ease with calling out her peers, she is unable to identify any antiracist action aside from cultural consumption. Given the dominance of Melamed's (2011) official antiracisms of the 20th century, where consuming narratives of racial others itself functions as antiracist action, this struggle is not surprising. While this can be a place to start, that she seems unable to come up with other action is notable.

Similarly, Ali struggled to articulate what antiracism could look like in her life:

> I'm trying to think of ways I would have to change something about my life. I don't feel like I go about my day and I'm racist—I feel like I kind of just go throughout my day. I don't feel like I could pinpoint one thing about my day, like there's that one thing I would change.

Ali's struggle to see beyond how she might be racist as she goes about her day demonstrates how an individualist view of racism, central to WPP, dead-ends when it comes to antiracism. Other participants were able to name how schoolings' official antiracisms (e.g., understanding racism as racial slurs) fell short, alleviating some of the personal responsibility for struggling to address racism, "I know in class I'm so stuck on the side, because just my entire life I was thinking like, oh to not be, it's like don't say racist things."

These participants understood the limitations of White privilege pedagogy, yet they did not have access to other models of antiracism. Moreover, their models of racism and Whiteness seemed to get in the way of antiracist possibilities. Specifically, the worse they believed racism to be (itself a mark of good nonracist Whiteness), the less possible antiracism became. In a way, determining racism as a solvable issue might suggest a failure to recognize its terrible scale. These positions might then perform a dual function: participants simultaneously affirm the severity and importance of racism as a problem while excusing their personal inaction. They also, significantly, represent the logical conclusion of participants' education on race and racism, which emphasizes the severity of racism potentially at the expense of the antiracist positions available to young White people, as Maria observed. This also represents a bind, wherein recognition of the severity and intransigence of racism is demanded of young people, who are then charged to take up antiracism, typically without direction, as their personal responsibility. Young White people must think of racism as concurrently intractable and personally remediable.

Moreover, not only are students to feel bad and do nothing, students who take up WPP are being "good" by following the official guidelines of the classroom. In contrast with the potential for resistance to lead to antiracism, taking up WPP seems to align with being a good nonracist White person, like the "assimilationists" of history (Kendi, 2016). By discouraging resistance and celebrating official curriculum, to say nothing of call-out culture, WPP can push students to cycle back to ineffectual, good nonracism of official antiracisms. As Leonardo and Zembylas (2013) wrote, "To the non-racist, it is something one is; to the anti-racist, it is something one does" (p. 156). In my own classroom, insofar as WPP was official curriculum, *being* antiracist by taking up WPP could even result in better grades! Antiracist work that addresses and shifts these constructs can have a significant effect on young White people's antiracist practice. As Ben observed, "My sense is that there are more people, maybe far more, who are less inclined to take action or will take less action because the problem feels insurmountable."

BEN FEELS HE HAS ALWAYS ALREADY FAILED AT ANTIRACISM

Having taken up the difficult knowledges presented by White privilege pedagogy without empathetic consumption of films and texts like *The Help* (Taylor, 2011), Ben represents a second possible position alongside Heidi. Ben seemed sensitive to the concerns raised earlier and positioned himself outside of the in/out binary of WPP. He also rejected potential identification with and objectification of the subject of that shame by arguing that service learning can be, as he put it, "dancing on the ashes." Yet despite his keen insight into how shame hindered his pursuit of antiracism, he seemed no closer to taking up antiracist action than other participants.

He and I spent several conversations exploring this. Ben took up shame and race within his senior research project, where he explored how unexamined shame allows racism to persist, suggesting that, as he put it, "A national examination of shame would overcome White supremacy." He explained:

> Unexamined shame comes from like, this is speaking from my experience. The shame, you feel like [he snaps] when someone is like talking about race and you feel like you can't engage with this person or in this discussion because, um, whether, well for a myriad of reasons, like I don't have the vocabulary to, I'm White so I can't, everything I could say has already been said, they won't understand me, they won't understand where I'm coming from. . . . I was never like, or for the longest time, I didn't really have the vocabulary to talk about that stuff and that was kind of why I didn't. And so, I didn't have the vocabulary, so I felt ashamed about that, so I didn't contribute. And I didn't contribute, so I felt ashamed about that so I didn't contribute again and it was, like, a positive feedback loop.

Ben described feeling like he had always already failed at antiracism, and that that sense of failure is durable. Shame both preceded and followed his failures to take up antiracism. His sense of having failed at antiracism leaves him ashamed, and his shame inhibits him from taking up antiracism. I believe the loop he describes is common among other liberal White participants and helps explain the boundedness they experienced. For example, Ali's paradoxical sense that "There's something right in front of me that I know I should do, but I don't know what that is," or Jenny's "There isn't much I can do, but there is," becomes sensible in this model. A shame feedback loop could be a natural result of taking up difficult knowledges within White privilege pedagogy, which encourages feelings of guilt and responsibility without directing White people beyond those feelings toward action.

In my second conversation with Ben a week later, we continued to explore how shame intersects with his antiracism. Specifically, we discussed his attendance at St Ann's as a privilege about which he felt ashamed. Our conversation laid out the process by which he became bound within shame and is worth quoting at length. Ben began by clarifying that his decisions are always contextual:

> *Ben:* I feel like something that I never communicated is that I am very much a product of my upbringing and very much a product of like media, the media I consumed. So the parties I align with, the people I aligned with. I don't know. I'm no, I do the things that I don't like sometimes. . . . Most people see that mold that like, that they're born in, that they're a product of, that they exist as, they see that as like, any effort to push them out of that is like a, even by themselves, is an act of hatred.
>
> *Kevin:* Mm. What's an example of that?
>
> *Ben:* Hmm. So [12-second pause] . . .
>
> *Kevin:* I don't think you're wrong.
>
> *Ben:* Yeah, I want to find a good example. So if I, think to myself, um, me going to school here is like the product of a racist system. Which, I know it is, but also I have a responsibility to myself and my mom to go here because she has sacrificed a lot for me to go here. And, um, it could be good for me. . . . So, and sometimes it feels like, like to push me out of that, like, headspace, my justification for coming here and it seems like it's an attack on me, not as an attack on my actions . . .
>
> *Kevin:* So the hatred part is, you have questions about or concerns about attending the school for the Whiteness, the racism, all that. Um, [breath] uh, so, but that can feel like an attack on you, because you're here and you're getting things out of it.
>
> *Ben:* Yes . . .
>
> *Kevin:* And that that's kind of um, awful to feel. [laughter]
>
> *Ben:* Yeah. And rather than, I think it's usually the side, that the side that's motivated to attack me is this side that offers what some would say is the only way to relieve, the only true way to relieve that self-hatred.
>
> *Kevin:* Which is . . .
>
> *Ben:* Humanization through deconstruction of racism.
>
> *Kevin:* Okay. So what would that look like in this specific case?
>
> *Ben:* Me wanting to go to a public school because it is genuinely better than this school. Actually. I don't know what genuinely better means.

K: Let's stick with you wanting to go to another school. So you haven't done that.

Ben: I've not gone to another school. I want . . .

Kevin: I assume you're probably not going to do that before you graduate. So here you are, you have an option, which has its own complications of course. And you don't take it.

Ben: Yes.

Kevin: What does that feel like?

Ben: It feels [8-second pause], feels like, dammit, I've thought about this so many times. I've just, feel like it's not desensitized, but it's something different. I just feel, like my gut is like, "Well, I'm going here."

Kevin: So yeah, that makes . . .

   [crosstalk]

Ben: Apathy.[1]

Kevin: A lot of sense.

Ben: Apathy.

Kevin: But that, does it, is that a shift in you? Apathy that comes after some, uh, self-antagonism?

Ben: Yes.

Kevin: Okay. What else? Where else does the apathy, what else is the apathy masking or covering or treating?

Ben: Um, hmm [18-second pause; I make a note]. My inability in—my past failures to address racism.

In short, the shame Ben describes about his ongoing privilege (i.e., his accrual of the spoils of White supremacy) could only be mitigated by an act of self-hatred, acting against his and his mother's interest. This impasse leaves him in a familiar apathy, as in, he always already feels ashamed of his inaction. In this exchange, I was not satisfied that "apathy" was the ultimate result of not taking up the antiracist possibilities he encountered. Ben was not an apathetic person, and I suspected that his apathy was doing important work. Indeed, his apathy served as an anesthetic for his "past failures to address racism," protecting him from feeling like a hypocrite or bad person for not only failing at antiracism, but *continuing to fail* at antiracism.

Further, that he describes attempting to push oneself out of the mold they're born into functions as an "act of hatred" aligns with Thandeka's (2001) exploration of White shame. For Thandeka, White identity development involves the creation and maintenance of internal and external "non-white zones" policed by familial and social acceptance. Moving beyond Whiteness, then, threatens that acceptance by invoking shame. Yet the shame explored by Thandeka is rooted in external shame, invoked by family or caregivers, and while Ben mentions that his potential move to a public school could negatively impact his mother, it is his desire to attend the public school "because it is *genuinely* better," that constitutes what he calls "humanization through the deconstruction of racism." I passed over this in our conversation, yet its contrast with Thandeka's work with shame is notable. Transferring to a public school is not enough. Ben suggests that he must *believe* that the school is a better option for him, implying that what must be different is not only his external situation but his internal one. His shame is rooted not only in his failure to take up antiracism, but also in his failure to be a certain kind of antiracist. Even his motivations were suspect. His commitment to antiracism had to be total, inside and out, or he failed. Ben noticed and attempted to resist this totalizing mentality: "Purity is nonexistent. I feel like I've come to that conclusion in other spaces but not this one. I feel like up until now it's sort of been like, I've had to accept all of it or none of it." Ultimately, his sense of shame is self-imposed.

This is another example of how these participants' experiences and understandings of race talk are meaningfully different than the literature. For example, Matias (2016) pushes Thandeka further: "If in whiteness the ideal self is one that internalizes narcissism, entitlement, and false racial kinship with other Whites, then nothing is more shameful than when that false ideal is threatened by reality" (p. 88). This was absolutely not the case here. Ben's shame came from his struggle to repudiate that Whiteness in the right way; he likely would have welcomed a reality that definitively threatened that Whiteness. Additionally, the participants evinced none of the redemption Margolin (2015) critically attributed to the profession of White privilege. For Margolin, White people declaring their White privilege was a way to *maintain* rather than abdicate their Whiteness. Rather, the shame several articulated came not from a recognition of their White privilege but from their failure to enact the antiracism they felt was their responsibility. It was not that these participants had outgrown these models, but that the models did not seem to apply at all.

BOUNDEDNESS

For Ben to both attend St. Ann's and not attend St. Ann's to fulfill his idea of being good (as a son and as an antiracist), is a double-bind. If he leaves, he risks feeling shame for letting down his mom, though not because of Whiteness. If he stays, he risks feeling shame for not being antiracist. The bind leaves him feeling, as he described, apathy, which serves as a salve for his anxieties and shame. Again, Ben and other participants did not seem ashamed of being White; they seemed ashamed of having always already failed at antiracism.

There were multiple contradictory injunctions about antiracism that left participants in binds. I highlighted several of these in the previous chapters. Some arose from assumptions shared by participants, including we must fix racism, racism is too large and complicated to be fixable; we can't be positive that an antiracism action is justified, we must be justified to take antiracism action; we can only talk about race and racism with people who are "in," it only helps to talk about race and racism with people who are "out;" and we can only participate in race talk when we are certain of ourselves, we cannot be certain of ourselves within race talk. Others were shared explicitly by participants, including we must understand the experiences of POC to fix racism, we cannot fully understand the experiences of POC; we must be experts to address racism without harming others, we cannot be experts about racism; we cannot talk about race and racism with other White people only, we cannot talk about race and racism with POC; we need to teach race and racism when kids are young, we cannot teach race and racism to young kids; we can't stay White, we can't be any other race; and finally shame and guilt motivate us to talk and not talk about race, to act and not act.[2]

As if these were not enough, Ben observed that even his motivation for practicing antiracism was suspect: "I mean, to a certain extent you're—I work on race for myself because it humanizes me. This is another thing I've thought a lot about, like, like whether it's bad, if I work on race, like if I think about race primarily for myself." That participants were caught up in so many binds surprised me. I had not looked for nor anticipated this, but the binds were unavoidable. I was also not prepared for how fraught antiracism would be, or that so many participants with seemingly sincere antiracist beliefs would be so lost trying to take it up. I believe double-bind theory alongside emerging research on trauma can help explain this.

Double-bind theory was originally proposed as an explanation for schizophrenic behavior by psychiatrist Gergory Bateson in the 1950s (Gibneyt, 2006).[3] While no longer thought of in this context, it remains a powerful discursive construct, and it remains crazy-making.

Double-binds can be understood in basic terms using the context of White privilege pedagogy in a classroom:

1. You must accept your responsibility for racism; you are racist.
2. If you don't accept this, it is because you are resisting, and thus racist.
3. You cannot point out this contradiction. If you do, you are resisting, and thus racist.
4. You can't leave the situation.

Further, and more insidiously, "the context is organized by the avoidance of punishment which usually take the form of withdrawal of love, the expression of hate or anger and other manifestations of the principal theme of abandonment" (Gibneyt, 2006, p. 50). For Bateson, the avoidance of punishment and withdrawal of love took place within the context of family systems. What carries over, especially in the classroom, are the power dynamics underlying this, "the double binds 'work' because someone has power over someone else, or at very least (and hardly 'least'), someone has the right to define the operant context for another person" (p. 55). The operant context, in this case, is White privilege pedagogy.[4]

STUCK WITHIN GUILT AND SHAME

White participants discussing race and antiracism experience guilt and shame is hardly a new concept. Further, these feelings do not typically translate into antiracist action (Lensmire et al., 2013). Yet more is happening here. Linder's (2015) observation about shame in her own study participants hearkens calling out and is helpful here:

> Feelings of guilt and shame are commonly associated with white identity development, but the participants in this study described the ways in which their guilt and shame fueled their fear of appearing racist, resulting in inaction related to antiracist work. (p. 544)

These young White people certainly feared appearing racist, yet their inaction also seemed informed by their feelings of guilt and shame themselves, outside of the fear of appearing racist. Feeling shame itself seemed to limit participants' ability to even *think* about race and seemed innate to the topic itself, as though they were always already positioned as guilty or ashamed when the topic was raised. As noted earlier, Banks (2016) discovered that "thoughts about racial and ethnic groups are so engrained in American society via anger" that overt political appeals are not necessary; being angry was enough to reinforce a political belief (p. 637). I suspect there are similar mechanisms at work with guilt and shame.

In the same way the racial discourses explored in Chapter 3 confounded participants' efforts to take up antiracism, the emotion of race talk, specifically guilt and shame, left participants feeling stuck. While participants were able to identify potential avenues of antiracism, their struggles to take them up dominated our conversations. Jenny followed her comment "There's not much I can do, but there is" by adding, "You feel like guilty for not doing anything but you want to do something." Similarly, Ali struggled to feel effective at antiracism, saying, "There's always something more to be done? There's always that like, you know when you leave and you forgot something, like you know when you need to go on a trip and you're like, I forgot something. It's kind of like that to me." Ali also shared that she felt guilty when she didn't notice something someone else called out as racist, as though, like Ben, she needed to recognize every possible problematic thing to properly take up antiracism and assuage that guilt. In fact, Ali's anxiety to catch every instance is indicative of antiracism as something we *are*, rather than something we practice. Another way to say that is within this model a person can try and *fail*, and in failing, be racist, rather than *practice* antiracism. When it comes to antiracism, this is an unhelpful model to say the least, a paralysis rooted in individualism and animated by shame.

These feelings of being stuck or inadequate were common among the more liberal participants and seemed central to both participants' available antiracisms and their sense of themselves as good people. To make better sense of this problem, I turn back to Ben, who articulated feeling stuck a bit more clearly than other participants. For example, he said:

> I consume media that encourages that sort of, ideal, like with those sort of ideas that people should be not only aware of their race but race, power, sex, that they should be, but they should be always trying to diffuse it. . . . But at the same time, they sort of mean like, or I sort of perceived that I should be ashamed of [pause] like at *every* single instance where I'm not actively diffusing it. I don't know. I don't know what I'm saying. It's hard. It's hard to place.

While still caught in it, Ben was able to externalize this stuckness expressed by Ali and Jenny. Not only did he feel he ought to be working against oppressive systems, but that, like Ali, any moment in which he was *not* working against those systems was shame worthy. I too have felt overwhelmed by what feels like an obligation toward shame, that my goodness as a person of privilege depended on my moment-to-moment abdication of that privilege.

Complicating this further, Ben struggled with shame in that he experienced it, knew it wasn't helpful, but also felt obligated to maintain it. "But at the same time I sort of don't want to, just because I feel like if I get rid of it completely, I just, I won't be motivated to not be racist." This view was shared by several participants, despite how when participants spoke about what actually shifted their views, personal conversations (Maria, Ali), or fact finding (David) helped them change, rather than shame.

Ben and I also sorted out that the antiracist action he ought to take up was obscured by his lack of certainty over what exactly that should be:

> *Ben:* I believe that it's an impossible task for me to be this [pause] sorta to be constantly aware, and it shouldn't be, I don't know, I'm conflicted. . . . Because I don't know. I couldn't be constantly secure that everything I was doing is justified. Okay. Yes. I cannot do that.
> *Kevin:* Right, but in order to not feel shame for being White . . .
> *Ben:* I need to constantly be justified.
> *Kevin:* Yeah. Well, that's a bind, isn't it?
> *Ben:* It is a bind.

For Ben, that he contributes to (and feels ashamed of) those racist, sexist, classist patterns is as unavoidable as his Whiteness. That he contributes to these patterns is consistent with critical pedagogy (Kumashiro, 2002). That he needed those feelings to take up antiracism, or that his antiracist actions must be constantly justified, however, are not. Yet both are typical of the emotional positionality of several participants who shared what seemed like forbiddingly difficult standards for their antiracism. This is a problem. Further, while I'm not sure what Ben meant by "media" that encouraged him to be "always trying to diffuse" his privileges, I wonder how a pedagogy focused on instilling a sense of the horror of racism without any clear actionable changes has contributed to this. I wonder if his feeling stuck in shame is exactly what White privilege pedagogy invites him to feel.

*   *   *

I explore shame and double-bind theory to better understand the context in which young White people are choosing whether to take up antiracism. I believe it can help us recognize how we as teachers and our students can get in our own way. I have struggled to make sense of resistant White students outside of a framework that positions them as "attached to their Whiteness" in ways substantially at odds with their peers. Making better sense of the social and emotional contexts can create space for exploration where there had only been space for judgment. Double-bind theory similarly "does not 'blame' the family nor the parents, nor does it imply malicious, deliberate intent to those involved in the communicational maze" (Gibneyt, 2006, p. 51). The solution to double-bind problems, relevant to teachers as the inadvertent perpetuators of them, is to avoid creating them in the first place.

Guilt and shame themselves were thus a messy constellation of mutable boundaries and unspoken rules around race for these liberal White young people. In particular, the liberal participants' sense of themselves as antiracist seemed closely linked to these feelings, as if feeling shame in and of itself indicated that they were doing the right thing. Zembylas (2013) helps to locate this dynamic within recent pedagogies:

> More importantly though, it has been argued that the discourse of critical pedagogy establishes and maintains its own disciplinary affects; that is, it functions as a 'pedagogy of affect'[5] that mobilizes dominant tropes, especially in anti-racist pedagogies. These dominant tropes are associated with certain affects such as commitment, devotion, and faith that may become normalized and even repressive. In other words, if these affects are not present among teachers or students in the context of critical pedagogy, then an anti-racist pedagogy may be considered a failure. (p. 178)

In other words, feeling bad within the context of White privilege pedagogy, or perhaps more accurately *appearing to feel bad* through affective performance, about racism can both indicate and constitute antiracism; if you don't seem ashamed of yourself, you're doing it wrong and deserve censure. As Trainor also recognized, the stuckness of our White students is, in part, a function of our own pedagogy. Good nonracist White students are to confess their privilege as a performance of empathy led by shame: the better the good White student, the more durable the shame. Again, I took this up myself as a classroom teacher in a race to the bottom, where the worse everyone seemed to feel, the better I was doing.

Moreover, Zembylas is addressing a failure of pedagogy, where students and teachers could hold the pedagogy responsible. For these participants, the pedagogy, however imperfect, was not ultimately a failure; *they* were. This indicates an increasingly challenging emotional load on young White people. Further, the more participants took up WPP, the more they seemed to link the affects of guilt and shame to antiracism. In fact, insofar as WPP has been official curricula, students could perform shame and guilt to earn better grades. On top of that, shame and guilt, like schooling itself, often function individually, so that each good White person wrestled within these binds on their own. It is little wonder liberal White students struggled to take up antiracism. The conservative participants, less beholden to WPP, did not seem as bound in this way.

CONCLUSION

The previous two chapters have posed race talk as a set of problems needing new or different analysis, including historical and social perspectives that reframe raced discourses in more helpful ways. Given the opportunity to step outside of the rules that govern classroom race talk in the context of the work, these young White people spoke persuasively, if self-consciously, about their misgivings about available discourses of race talk. They articulated the shortcomings of referential language, the hypocrisy of calling out, and the inadequate social and academic support they had around race and racism. This chapter poses problems more directly related to emotion and identity and have consequently been less visible in classroom discourses. Like the flawed discourses in Chapters 3 and 4, these emotional structures are energized by the status quo of Whiteness and White supremacy; in other words, to White people they *feel* like the right things to do, despite their counterproductivity. Within a construct of guilt and shame, to permit themselves to feel the wrongness of their shame and stuckness implied that they *themselves* were wrong. These young White people, perhaps because of the nature of shame, or perhaps because of the personal nature of emotion or antiracist action, struggled to critique these structures with the same clarity as they did referential language or calling out. We are left to wonder how their White guilt and shame insulated them from taking up more generative antiracisms.

The messiness of shame articulated by Ben and felt by the more liberal participants is a problem calling for more nuanced understandings and interpretations. In mainstream psychology, that shame is a negative referent is a slam dunk; nothing good can come from believing oneself to be inherently bad. Yet feminist scholarship, along with recent sense-making about the appeal of Donald Trump's apparent shamelessness, offer new perspectives and possibilities for working within shame in pursuit of White antiracist action. The shame and stuckness explored in this chapter, despite being less visible in classroom race talk, was deeply felt by White participants and is deeply resonant for me. In the following chapter, I explore recent scholarship and thinking about the social and pedagogical possibilities of shame, the role of and remedy for White racial trauma, as well as new understandings of empathy and witnessing.

CHAPTER 6

Shame, Trauma, and Empathy

Let's face it, we're undone by each other. And if we're not, we're missing something.

—Judith Butler

In "Melancholy Whiteness," Kate Manne (2018) explores the role of shame in Whiteness and Whiteness's potential for antiracism. She poses, based on the work of Judith Butler, what she calls "a very general problem: how to break the news to the historically privileged of their shameful, ongoing legacy, e.g., colonialism, White Supremacy, and racism, without inducing the kind of shame that seeks an irrevocable break between the self and the other—or, simply, to break one or the other, if not both, of these subjects" (p. 233). I will work through this question, with help from Manne and others, in this chapter. If WPP sought to invoke self-examination from White people in pursuit of antiracism, perhaps our work going forward is how to undergo that self-examination effectively, without the paralyzing "breaks" Manne names and that are evidenced in the previous chapter. Moreover, in the same way Whiteness and White supremacy become more sensible with the more accurate historical and sociological contexts explored in Chapter 2, new emotional and psychosocial perspectives can help us better understand and work through the stucknesses and boundednesses described in Chapter 5. This chapter will touch on pedagogical possibilities within shame, trauma, and empathy, each of which operate as ways of being in relationship with the self and other. These topics each deserve much more consideration than I have space for here. I hope to bring them into this conversation about Whiteness and antiracism to recognize those possibilities and provide a direction for future work.

STUCKNESS AND SHAME

So far, Thandeka's (2001) work has informed most of my working
through the shame I encountered in my classroom (as well as in my
personal journey as a White person). As a reminder, Thandeka argued
that shame structured the process of Whitening for young White people, whose caregivers generated (explicitly or not) internal and external
White and non-White zones. To transgress those boundaries threatened rejection from the caregiver, and to abide the boundaries meant
shamefully forfeiting human companionship and interdependence. A
young White person then had to choose to remain safely within the
love of their caregivers by relinquishing their friendships and interests. Shame reoriented White people away from interracial solidarity and toward White caregivers and authority figures. In this model,
race talk itself existed in carefully policed non-White zones, where a
young White person could alienate their caregivers or friends by breaking social codes of Whiteness. As earlier chapters explored, White and
non-White spaces include a broad range of social, political, emotional,
economic, and geographic categories so that "being White" includes
everything from musical preference to neighborhood, from diet to how
a person spends their weekends. These social boundaries and the external shame-based pressures that maintain them have become more visible in recent years, which perhaps explains why participants no longer
seemed as caught within them. Thandeka's shame construct has been
central to the ways critical Whiteness has taken up shame.

Meanwhile, WPP represents a second shame construct at work
within White people. It has demanded that young White people confess to their shameful White privileges and that their failure to do
so means that they are racist and shameful. This shame also operated externally by policing the language and professed beliefs of
White people. As I explored in Chapter 5, the participants' race talk
seemed to be closely associated with shame, as evidenced by the litany
of binds they encountered when trying to make sense of racism as
White people. Participants described and acted out ways that shame,
being better than or worse than, was central to their encounters with
race talk as White people. Moreover, for more liberal participants, a
sense of shame or feeling bad about racism indexed their goodness as
White people both externally and internally. Yet as Ben noted (and I
agreed), while this shame *felt* necessary, it wasn't welcome or generative. I argued that his and other participants' shame might contribute
to their paralysis, and that the more conservative participants (Ryan,

David, or Ken) more easily imagined antiracist possibilities precisely because they had rejected the shame liberal Whiteness attaches to being White. Beyond Thandeka, constructs of Whiteness (in this case good nonracist Whiteness), bound the actions and ways of being of young White people through shame.

These young White people, along with so many others, remain undeniably and profoundly affected by the shame attendant to being White in our White supremacist society. I believe shame operates at the heart of Whiteness, and our sense-making of that process has been and will remain central to antiracism. Given the centrality of shame in White people's experiences of race and antiracism, can shame be generatively applied to the problem of their antiracism? In the following section, I will explore new ways of understanding the role of shame within Whiteness and antiracism.

Recent literature (Hochschild, 2016; Isenberg, 2016) have sought to make sense of Whiteness and White resistance in the (White) shadow of the presidency of Donald Trump. They each work through Whiteness in helpful ways, though they each tend to focus on the sympathies, evasions, and resistances of those on the political right, ostensibly or explicitly for the edification of the left. As a White person studying Whiteness, I was often asked about these books with the suggestion that the new project of the left was to make sense of reactionary Whiteness using an analysis of Trumpism. I was deeply curious about the Whiteness operating within Trumpism, though my curiosity was detached and arrogant. It rarely extended beyond my own judgmental sense of superiority to, for example, the way my Whiteness mirrored the Whiteness of those who followed him. Outside of that superiority, Trumpism and his shamelessness especially made little sense to me.

Similarly, Donovan Schaefer (2019) explores the mechanisms of Whiteness and shame within Trumpism. He argues that shame and the repudiation of shame are central to understanding Trumpism and, consequently, political alignment and Whiteness. He describes it this way:

> Shame on the move—an openness to shame, a trafficking in shame—is how left-wing politics feels. Leftists use shame to challenge not only the politics of others, but also themselves, grinding away their own sense of comfort in a relentless project to become more sensitive, more thoughtful, more moral. The modern American progressive political project is heavily keyed to this internal disciplinary apparatus. (pp. 6–7)

If this sounds hyperbolic, recall the ways WPP structured evaluation and grades according to how a student did or did not take up White privilege, insofar as it was official curriculum. Schaefer, with the help of Eve Sedgwick, goes on to work through the ways political correctness acted, very much like White privilege I would add, as "a pedagogy, a sweeping masterwork of shame designed to rip residual structures of degradation from speech," which in turn "provoke[d] a shame response, a furious refusal of culpability" (p. 7). Threatened White racial superiority, in an effort to remain innocent to the moral judgment by or on behalf of racial groups they consider insurgent, have taken up Trump's shamelessness. Schaefer convincingly details not only Trump's policies and speeches, but his mannerisms, such as never looking down, or never laughing, that operate as "a dyad of shame and dignity, often organized around race" (pp. 7–8). Trump's wall (importantly paid for by Mexico), his Muslim ban, his absolute refusal to apologize to anyone for anything in any context, and his scathing critique of Obama's famous 2009 apology in Cairo as a shameful show of weakness, all operate as offering dignity in the face of shame. "Trump is the vindicator, a scion of defiance and his slogan *Make America Great Again* represents a perfect encapsulation of the affective dynamics that animate his entire campaign—a transition from a state of ignominy to a state of glory" (p. 8).

Schaefer argues convincingly that political resentment does not fully explain Trump's appeal; rather, Trump offers White Americans respite from the threat of being victimized by racialized humiliation. "One avoids humiliation of loss and victimage by humiliating the other, by diminishing their status and capacity, destroying their sense of pride, reducing them to a lower state of being" (Gossberg, as quoted in Schaefer, 2019, p. 7). For Schaefer, Trump is making political hay with the same anxious repudiation of White racial shame taken up by George Wallace in the 1960s. In other words, because Trump redirects shameful feelings at racial Others, shame is essential to Trumpian Whiteness. In response to the decline of White majorities, Whiteness as normal and unmarked, and especially in response to the pedagogies of shame from the left, Trump allowed and encouraged White people to feel good by naming racial Others as bad.

The history of Whiteness told in Chapter 2 shows that this strategy is as old as Whiteness itself. Yet even as I recognized Trump's base as scapegoating others to redirect their own White shame, I continued to believe that they *ought* to be ashamed, that their attachment to White pride or American nationalism or, charitably, their White innocence, was shameful. I was, and am, not alone in this belief.

I should clarify that even as I developed my consciousness around the working of Whiteness explored in this book, this belief remained imprinted in the back of my mind. Even as I explore it now, I can feel its attractive suggestion: I, by comparison, am better than they are. By positioning myself as better than, as more woke or as further ahead, I have been able to avoid the ways my Whiteness was the same as theirs and fail to appreciate how their redirection could help me be more present to my own. I have been insensible to *my own* White shame; my own ego, damaged by Whiteness, remains susceptible to feeling a superiority made permissible by woke politics because it is superior to other White people. Moreover, as a teacher of White students, my work to foster antiracist awareness, particularly students who appear to be resistant to antiracism, is inhibited by my investment in their shortcomings. As I wrote in the introductory chapter, I *needed* those students to resist both to enact my reactive pedagogy, and to affirm my position as the good White teacher. So long as I failed to address my own shame-based sense of superiority, my antiracist pedagogy was as stuck as my participants. My liberal White friends share in this struggle, both to articulate how that superiority operates and to move beyond it.

Perhaps another way to observe this dynamic is through the tendency of the White people I've worked with (and myself) to over-identify the racism of others as inhibiting our own antiracism possibilities. In education, this looks like blaming administrators, other teachers, or even students for antiracist shortcomings, or by positioning oneself as more or less "woke," or as being ahead or behind on a linear journey to antiracism. While I did not often hear the young White people in my work name being better than, David and Joel noted this tendency among more liberal White people. David especially might note the hypocrisy of Democrats identifying Republicans as racist without a savvy read on how easily Republicans can identify Democrats the same way. Further, I wonder if it is possible to read participants' shame at being White as a form of being "worse than," by comparison, BIPoC folks. Certainly the right has leveled this accusation within its criticism of "woke" pedagogies.

For both the left and right, for those taking up and those skeptical of WPP, shame is a powerful and poorly understood operant. In some ways, the fundamental and unavoidable work of addressing Whiteness must start with attending to the inherent shame of being and having to become White in a White supremacist society. Black scholars, especially James Baldwin, Toni Morrison, and Thandeka, have known and articulated the ways Whiteness emotionally handicaps White people (as Mills's [1997] Racial Contract morally handicaps White people). I and other Whiteness scholars have recently wrestled with how to navigate this. We know that dividing White people by who is more or less racist dodges the deeply personal antiracist work of unpacking internalized Whiteness and White supremacy (Lensmire, 2017). We also know to take seriously the work of unpacking and working through that shame (Lee-Nichols & Tierney, 2018; Lensmire, 2017). Still, we are left with a model of shame that is as unavoidable as it is unhelpful. A renewed attention to shame can begin by framing it more helpfully using the following models.

HOW THIS HELPS

First, we can reconsider the effect of shame by understanding the shame of being White as, in part, what Zembylas (2019) calls a shame at being human. Based on the work of Primo Levi, Lévinas, and other scholars who wrote about the holocaust of WWII, he describes "the shame of being a witness to a crime of unimaginable scale, the shame one feels for being unable to have done anything to have prevented the unthinkable," and "the emergence of ethical responsibility despite the inability to prevent wrongs" (pp. 304–305). This is not a shame of being unworthy to oneself or in the eyes of others, but rather a sense of complicity, however abstract, in the suffering of Others. Zembylas's exploration of this shame helps make sense of several aspects of White antiracist work, and is worth quoting at length:

> As Lévinas writes about responsibility and shame in relation to the horrors of the Second World War and the Shoah, "My being-in-the-world or my 'place in the sun', my being at home, have these not also been the usurpation of spaces belonging to the other man whom I have already oppressed or starved, or driven out into a third world; are they not acts of repulsing, excluding, exiling, stripping, killing?" Shame, for Lévinas, then, is founded upon the solidarity with others, which obliges us to open up to the Other and take responsibility to respond before the face of the suffering Other. In this sense, explains Guenther, "the ethical shame which the Other provokes in me does not make me feel stuck to

myself; rather, it opens a way of *getting un-stuck* from my own suffocating relation to being." (p. 308)

I'm reminded of Ben's sense of discomfort at his privilege to return to his expensive school while the man he talked with at the shelter remained there. I have felt this as well; who am I to own my nice house in my safe neighborhood? Who am I to live my privileged life? Lévinas's description applies to the sense of shame evinced by liberal White people at not only the fact of their White privileges, but at their inability to do much about them. Lévinas proposes that this shame has the potential to align me *with*, rather than separate me from, the lives of Others.

However, as Zembylas later warns, if I recognize the intolerable crime and my ethical responsibility without also taking action to address that crime, the "shame at being human" I experience in the context of my Whiteness does not feel like an ethical shame that can foster solidarity and will not open "a way of getting un-stuck" from my Whiteness. Rather, my shame at being human can become a personal shame in which I will feel stuck. I believe this is where so many of our young White people are stuck; they have been made aware of the monstrous crime of White supremacy yet are provided with little to no potential for corrective action. Without a construct of meaningful solidarity, they are stuck. However, when accompanied by action in solidarity, or at least the potential for action, shame can become a generative form of witnessing. As he explains, "To see the intolerable, then, is not enough; one must learn how to see the possibility for something else—for something that builds solidarity with Others" (p. 314).

In so far as my classroom work with White people has failed to imagine or generate racial solidarity, it has always been threatened by the stuckness of shame. Rather, I could make a move to shift away from that stuckness. I could address that shame directly, reframing it as an indicator of concern and as a call to action, whereupon my White students could, driven by their shame of being human, begin to imagine and create systems of racial solidarity. In short, I could make generative use of their White shame, rather than allowing that shame to function as a paralytic that leaves them stuck.

When my students experience that intense discomfort in the face of their complicity in Others' suffering, I must take care to temper both my tendency to comfort them, and my temptation to let them stew in their shame, to make them take their medicine. We are cautioned here to not move too quickly through shame and in doing so refuse the positive potential for antiracist motivation and engagement. If shame can allow us new possibilities, as Zembylas suggests, those new possibilities will emerge from the discomfort of shame, not from a superficial resolution of it. We are further cautioned to not pretend that shame, however positively inferred, is action in and of itself. And finally, whatever discomfort White people might experience from their shame, it remains a privileged experience from which White people can escape. Even so, I believe recognizing the positive potential of shame can better position White people to take up antiracism.

Second, we can and should address the White shaming of other White people. Common sense tells us that when Whiteness and its politics are animated by a desperate repudiation of shame, piling on more shame will only further entrench those politics. Ben recognized this imperative better than most, such as when he cautioned the group after sharing his instinct to refer to someone who denies White privilege as "what a fucking idiot." We can recognize the ways shame operates in both conservative and liberal White people. Both are unhelpful. Conservative and liberal political affiliation is, in the end, a superficial and largely unhelpful construct when it comes to antiracism. Moreover, Ben recognized the fallacy of assuming an open-mindedness among liberal White people. As he said, "What I value the most is just willingness to engage with me. And most people who are most willing to engage with me and have a good productive conversation, they're not liberal."

The problem of shaming other White people is not just that it is counterproductive, but that it traps us within shame constructs. To shame someone else is to traffic in shame, activating it within ourselves in order to direct it at someone else. Whether that is directed at racial Others (for conservative Whites) or White others (for liberal Whites), the mechanism is the same. When liberal White people feel a sense of superiority over other "less woke" White people, they are protecting themselves from the shame of their own wounded Whiteness *in the same way* conservative White people might feel a sense of superiority over racial Others. This is the lesson of the "in/out" groupings within Whiteness and echoes the caution of Black scholars like James Baldwin and Toni Morrison.

White people must stop shaming other White people, not only for the benefit of other White people, who typically reject such sentiments out of hand, but for their own benefit. Interrupting that cycle of shame can permit introspection, so that, for example, I can reflect on what I gain from my sense of superiority over others' cartoonish racism. By laughing at or feeling superior to the behavior of other White people, I mask my own ambivalent feelings and behaviors. Rather, White people can more generatively (and humanely) approach other White people with due humility, keeping in mind that all White people are subject to Whiteness even if that Whiteness manifests in seemingly contradictory ways. Likewise, in our political context, Zembylas (2020) calls for curiosity rather than derision, to examine *"how* peoples' affective attachments to Trump's politics are rooted in *both* feelings of anger and resentment (negative emotions) *and* the promise of redemption and hope (positive emotions)" (p. 161, emphasis in original). Liberal White people would do well to offer themselves and their own shame a similar curiosity. To that end, I return to Manne's work with shame and melancholy.

Manne (2018) takes seriously the stuckness White people feel in the face of the shameful legacy of Whiteness. Participants described encountering race talk and antiracism as having always already failed. Their shame was not borne, seemingly, of their *becoming* White, as Thandeka (2001) suggests. Rather, as Manne suggests, White people participate in the shameful legacy of White supremacy as a matter of course, and this matter-of-course enactment presents an unavoidable threat to White people's sense of themselves as good people. As participants pointed out, they should no longer be White, but they cannot be anything else. If Whiteness itself, an unavoidable way of being for White people, presents a threat to their sense of themselves as good people, of course they feel stuck in shame. They lacked a way of making sense of themselves as antiracist, and White privilege pedagogy did not provide one for them.

Manne (2018) explores melancholia[1] to help make sense of that stuckness. If mourning is about experiencing and processing loss, "melancholia involves a loss which is resisted rather than fully acknowledged. And it results in what might have been lost, or else regained, remaining not-quite-lost—be it a person, object, abstraction, ideal, or, in some cases, a cherished illusion" (p. 239). Manne suggests that, for some White people, facing themselves in the context of White supremacy is nearly unbearable. For those White people *any* acknowledgment of White culpability is furiously denied. That denial not only rejects shame and history; denying White privilege creates a cognitive dissonance that requires explanation and maintenance to sustain the "cherished illusion" in White innocence. This illusion can only be sustained by blaming the victims of oppression rather than oppression itself. Here, again, is Whiteness at work.

For Manne, White people's denial of being privileged (which they determine to be divinely or patriotically ordained, rather than socially conferred advantages) constitutes their melancholia. As she explains, "The denial or disavowal of a shameful historical legacy is an integral part of white ignorance; and such ignorance is bliss, a childish paradise, an Eden" (p, 239). While Manne's work focuses on the White denial of racism and White privilege, her description of the effect of that denial closely echoes the experiences of the more liberal participants who readily acknowledge their Whiteness:

> The melancholic person is hence in a kind of limbo—consigned to a state of perpetually losing. She hence cannot let go, and is forever *at* a loss— and at a loss to name the source of her sadness and ambivalence. The result, in Freud's view, is noisy self-abasement—the expression of an inward stripping away of the ego. (p. 239, emphasis in original)

For Manne, noisy self-abasement is the embrace of terms like *deplorables*, or waving the Confederate battle flag, both of which deny a "shameful historical legacy." For the liberal young White people in my classroom, confession and shame at their White privilege, along with their calling out of their less-woke peers, may have worked similarly. I wonder if their calling out served to preserve their sense of themselves as good people while holding at bay a full recognition of how that privilege functioned in their daily lives. In other words, we risk remaining invested in others' badness if we can only affirm our goodness by comparison. Shame is a construct of comparison, while healthy self-regard values the inherent goodness in all people, including the self. As Baldwin said, "I am not a n*****. I'm a man. But if you think I'm a n*****, it means you need it" (Peck, 2016). Our work is to cultivate a self-awareness that tolerates introspection, especially as we find ourselves outraged at the racism of others.

In the end, Manne (2018) offers a re-routing of the negative feelings of shame and melancholy similar to Zembylas:

> Shame is rendered tolerable by being wrought into a narrative that makes breaking with a shameful history a sign of character and integrity. . . . Obviously, it would be better if nobody needed to coddle the privileged, and lead them gently from darkness toward a mirror in flattering light. But sometimes, perhaps, it is necessary, to break through the melancholy

disavowals of shame that are not revolutionary, so much as violent and destructive. (pp. 240–241)

Again, she is addressing the violence and destruction of the political right whose antiracist work begins with the recognition of our shameful legacy. For the left, for me, for the presumed readers of this book, I suggest that whatever stuckness we experience might be tempered by our recognition that being stuck indicates that we are looking in the right places. The mechanisms of my disavowals of shame will look different than that of the right, but they are no less difficult, and they are no less of an impediment to progress. I believe we are stuck in similar ways and all in need of new ways of operating.

STUCKNESS AND TRAUMA

Like shame, making sense of and applying trauma frameworks to White people's race talk can offer helpful models for understanding student responses to antiracist pedagogies. Further, practices that mitigate the effects of trauma can be easily applied in the classroom and offer their own benefits. However, like shame, trauma calls for more space than is afforded here, and this treatment will be limited. Before I proceed, I want to caution that the racial traumas of people of color and those of White people are not comparable, and that discussing White racial traumas risks treating them as such. Moreover, White racial trauma as an antiracist concept raises several important concerns. First, I hesitate to use the language of trauma at all for several reasons, including that the language of trauma can essentialize complex experiences in unhelpful ways, and that applying the language of trauma can recall other examples of trauma, such as assault or genocide, suggesting comparability. Second, White trauma recenters Whiteness while threatening to overshadow the staggering racial trauma inflicted by White people on BIPoC communities. Finally, literature on racial trauma, particularly White racial trauma, are scant and recent, so this work cannot benefit from its own history.

So why engage with trauma at all? In a word, I found trauma frameworks unavoidable. Much of participant behavior and language around race talk aligned with the behavior and language of survivors of trauma. Additionally, Whiteness studies (especially Thandeka, 2001) locate the roots of White supremacy within

White racial trauma and call for it to be addressed. For example, in *Knowledge in the Blood*, Jansen (2009) explores the racial dynamics of pre- and post-apartheid South Africa as a Black academic whose career bridged both. He argues "that black and white South Africans came into democracy carrying traumatic memories of the apartheid past" (Chinoyowa, 2013, p. 93). Significantly, Jansen (2009) maintains that young South Africans, White and Black, each carry particular images of apartheid as knowledge in the blood, even if it ended years before they were born. For Jansen, these traumatic memories, which need not be personally experienced, persist in damaging ways for both Whites and Blacks. Like in the United States, some White South Africans maintained an identity of underdog, of resistance, during the height of apartheid, especially when confronted with potential racial equality.

I neither want to undervalue trauma as experienced by survivors of sexual abuse and assault or survivors of genocide nor can I dismiss the startling similarities evinced between White students discussing race and trauma survivors. Further, I believe the conceptual framework of trauma can help race theorists and classroom teachers better understand and address race talk. Perhaps most importantly, activities and exercises for accommodating, working through, and preventing trauma, such as breathing, visualization, and focusing exercises, have academic and social benefits for all of us.

Resmaa Menakem (2017), a race and social work scholar, takes up trauma in specifically racial contexts, exploring the racial experiences of Black bodies, police bodies, and White bodies. For Menakem, "white Americans have experienced this trauma in multiple ways. They watched others harm and kill Black bodies. They failed to prevent, stop, or challenge such attacks" (p. 101). In this way, White Americans' failure to take up antiracism itself can be a form of trauma, creating the paralyzing shame of having *always already failed* discussed earlier. Additionally, White people may experience pain when confronted with the reality of their racialized fear of Black bodies. Hamel (2019) described how the fear she may experience when encountering Black bodies leads to shame for experiencing that fear:

> If and when I experience fear in my white-body in the presence of Black-bodies, it is likely that I will also feel guilty and experience a strong sense of shame. It can be painful to observe and wonder what is happening in these instances and it is common for many white people to avoid, deny, and prevent this discomfort from happening. (p. 177)

These constitute a mounting emotional load on White students worth considering as we ask them to participate in race talk and can help us make sense of and work alongside White racial denial, professed ignorance, avoidance, as well as performances of wokeness. Once again, our task of examining and moving beyond these experiences must serve to address racism and anti-Blackness.

Menakem (2017) explains trauma as a defensive maneuver. "Trauma is the body's protective response to an event—or a series of events—that it perceives as potentially dangerous" (p. 7). We are traumatized when we experience something as "too much and too fast" and are unable to process or metabolize the event in real time. Bessel van der Kolk (2015) details how traumas can be retained within the mind and body and are then expressed in seemingly unlikely ways. He researched how engaging with the source or trigger of trauma can disengage Broca's area, the language center of the brain, as intense emotions from that experience come rushing back. A person experiencing this cannot therefore reason their way out of it. Rather, they are in thrall to their traumatic response, often not even aware that it is happening. Then, "after the emotional storm passes, they may look for something or somebody to blame for it" (p. 45). Further, van der Kolk explains how these feelings are largely beyond our control, and "as a result, shame becomes the dominant emotion and hiding the truth becomes the central preoccupation" (p. 67).

Ultimately, because it is located away from language within the mind and body, trauma is resistant to remedies focused on talking. As van der Kolk explains, "No matter how much insight and understanding we develop, the rational brain is basically impotent to talk the emotional brain out of its own reality" (p. 47). These dynamics, stumbling over words, ambivalences, attraction and revulsion, a struggle to articulate thoughts and feelings, and learned helplessness, have been readily observable in my students' race talk.

For young White people, I wonder if repeated exposure to WPP, combined with the various double-binds of race talk explored in Chapter 5, could contribute to these kinds of trauma responses. Moreover, the schooling environment, oriented almost entirely around talk, can be particularly poorly suited to respond. Because "recollection without affect almost invariably produces no result," the more we intellectualize racism the more we freeze it into place (van der Kolk, 2015 p. 184). As participants noted, schooling is routinely disembodied and disempowering, with students meant to sit quietly and passively in front of a teacher, and rarely permitted or encouraged to act. On this, Menakem (2017) offers a helpful direction:

> For the past three decades, we've earnestly tried to address white-body supremacy in America with reason, principles, and ideas—using dialogue, forums, discussions, education, and mental training. But the widespread destruction of Black bodies continues. . . . It's not that we've been lazy or insincere. But we've focused our efforts in the wrong direction. We've tried to teach our brains to think better about race. But white-body supremacy doesn't live in our thinking brains. It lives and breathes in our bodies. (p. 5)

An understanding of the traumas of becoming White and living within a White supremacist society can inform our classroom practices in helpful ways.

HOW THIS HELPS

van der Kolk's work with trauma aligns with and can help make sense of my White participants' struggles with race talk. The framework of trauma offers foundational models and strategies for mitigating the difficulties experienced by young White people in the context of race talk. For van der Kolk (2015), healing involves the following:

1. finding a way to be calm and focused,
2. learning to maintain that focus in response to images, thoughts, sounds, or physical sensations that remind you of the past,
3. finding a way to be fully alive in the present and engaged with the people around you,
4. not having to keep secrets from yourself, including secrets about the ways you have managed to survive. (pp. 205–206)

As he explains, these goals overlap and are best pursued in tandem. Similarly, Menakem (2017) suggests practicing mindfulness and self-soothing strategies when undertaking race work to help recognize and mitigate overwhelming self-protective measures our bodies enact in response to race talk. In other words, by building the capacity to engage in emotionally difficult work, White people strengthen their resilience to the workings of Whiteness that typically discourage sustained engagement. Finally, van der Kolk (2015) suggests that working against the secrecy and shame of trauma means "knowing what they know, and feeling what they feel" (p. 27). This reinforces the need to facilitate, cautiously and contextually, problematic race talk within White racial affinity groups.[2]

Practicing mindfulness and maintaining awareness of the emotional embodiment of race can help address the anxiety young White people described while potentially lessening the paralytic effect of the double-binds attendant to their race talk experiences. Before young people are confronted with the difficult knowledge of our racial history and present, our antiracist work would benefit from working to detoxify, though not necessarily make "safe," our classrooms.[3] Strategies developed to calm the autonomic nervous system for those struggling with trauma can also serve as effective tools for moderating White reactivity during conversations about race. While these are especially useful in guiding students through challenging conversations, we can all benefit from developing these practices.

Additionally, Menakem's (2017) distinction between what he calls clean and dirty pain can help us navigate challenging emotions. For Menakem, "dirty pain is the pain of avoidance, blame, and denial" taken up by those unwilling or unable to confront these struggles in a healthy way. Dirty pain only "create[s] more of it for themselves and others" (p. 20). I believe we can confidently label the shame-based maneuvers of Whiteness detailed earlier in this chapter as dirty pain. My classroom work with race talk has looked like struggling with the expressions of dirty pain, in particular defensiveness, denials, as well as the calling out and blaming, with little or no progress made. Even as I improved my practice in response to those maneuvers, dirty pain dodged, morphed, and reappeared. And of course it did: I was working with symptoms rather than causes.

Clean pain, on the other hand, is pain that is metabolized within our emotional selves and is expressed through vulnerability. For myself, I tend to articulate vulnerable feelings as judgments, as in "I feel attacked," rather than as an articulation of my emotional state, as in "I feel defensive." Even *writing* these statements feels different to me; "I feel attacked" orients me outward, while "I feel defensive" redirects me inward. This is the fundamental difference between clean and dirty pain. While dirty pain protects us by closing us off from the world, clean pain positions us as open, receptive, and ready to learn. I've struggled through challenging classroom conversations with dirty pain and occasionally with clean pain, though I did not have that language at the time. What I knew was the clear difference between when my students struggled against each other in conflict versus alongside each other in solidarity. The distinction between clean and dirty pain, or a process of opening and healing rather than one of defensiveness and closedness, can help us at least identify where we are and where we want to go.

van der Kolk's (2015) work with trauma draws similar conclusions about openness: "Communicating fully is the opposite of being traumatized" (p. 237). I wonder if this kind of open communication might be what participants had in mind when they called for "deeper conversations" among their peers about race. Additionally, van der Kolk recognizes the power of art, especially theater, to counter the paralysis of trauma:

> Trauma is about trying to forget, hiding how scared, enraged, or helpless you are. Theater is about finding ways of telling the truth and conveying deep truths to your audience. This requires pushing through blockages to discover your own truth, exploring and examining your own internal experience so that it can emerge in your voice and body on stage. (p. 337)

Several practitioners have embraced theater to better explore race, notably Tanner (2018) and Snyder-Young (2010). Boal's (1993) *Theater of the Oppressed*, which I've taken up in antiracism workshops as well as in my work with bullying, is similarly well suited to race work.

Finally, Menakem's (2017) *My Grandmothers Hands*, now a bestseller, operates as a workbook, with activities, prompts, and exercises, meant to offer a guide for a reader working through their own radicalized trauma. In my Whiteness work, both personally and in trainings, his guide has been invaluable in mapping out the pathway toward personal and interpersonal racial healing. His is not the only guide, and trauma is not the only framework, but they are readily available for folks ready to undertake the work. I take seriously his caution, and that of antiracist mindfulness practitioners like Ruth King (2018), that if we are serious about antiracism, we have to work from the inside out. As Menakem (2017) says, "We will not destroy White-body supremacy—or any other form of human evil—by trying to tear it to pieces. Instead, we can offer people better ways to belong and better things to belong to" (p. 149). In addition to shame and trauma, a renewed look at empathy allows White people new pathways to engaging in antiracism.

STUCKNESS AND EMPATHY

When I first encountered White privilege pedagogy, I understood my White privilege as my having more, more things, more money, more opportunities, while racial Others had less. This difference was driven home to me through books, movies, documentaries, and lectures where I was told personal accounts of BIPoC folks having less, of them struggling to get by while White people enjoyed a surfeit of these same things, a contrast heightened by these differences existing just across a highway or the tracks. I was to read these accounts and *feel for* those who had less. I was to put myself in their shoes, recognize how unfair it was, and then, presumably, work to change it (though this step was rarely addressed).

That WPP often results in the White consumption of the stories of cultural Others in the name of empathy raises concerns. Namely, Megan Boler (1999) cites the "untheorized gap between empathy and acting on another's behalf" (p. 157). For Boler, "passive empathy absolves the reader through the denial of power relations" (p. 161). This denial risks erasing the differences between people of color and Whites through an over-identification. It is one of several ways Whiteness serves to maintain White supremacy within the guise of progressive racial movements, in this case by cloaking White inaction with powerful yet unwarranted feelings of kinship with people of color.

Further, like Boler's (1999) concern regarding the self-focused responses generated by empathy, Zembylas (2006) cites how White Australians struggling with past mistreatment of aboriginal peoples can mobilize shame to ease their sense of isolation. "In other words, our shame *means* that we *mean well*. . . . Those who witness the past injustice through feeling 'national shame' are aligned with each other as 'well-meaning individuals'" (pp. 318–319, emphasis in original). I saw this dynamic with my White students as members of the "in" group aligned themselves against those who were "out" through calling out, side comments, and other complaints. Here again, "well-meaning" can act as a stand-in for antiracist action, allowing good nonracist White people to think of themselves as allies without actually doing anything. This relationship is a problem.

Boler is critical of the neoliberal empathy that resolves the suffering of others by eclipsing the reader within herself, cutting off access to what ought to hail the reader and call her to action. Rather, Boler calls for a more pointed empathy through testimonials, which implicate the listener in the struggle of the testifier. In this way, empathy shifts from a consumptive emotion that comforts to an outward facing emotion that discomforts. To better understand the role of empathy in high school, I'm going to focus on two common encounters students of privilege (in these examples, White students) have with Others, through service learning and multicultural classroom texts.

St Ann's was, through its mission statement as well as its practice, dedicated to issues of social justice. This commitment was visible in a number of ways, including a multitude of service opportunities both during and outside of school. Students had opportunities to help build housing, serve weekly meals in homeless shelters, and volunteer at a day care for low-income families. As part of their religion courses, all senior students spent a few hours each week doing "service," as it was called, at various service sites around town. These sites included crisis nurseries, shelters and drop-in centers for people experiencing home-lessness, schools in low-income neighborhoods, and hospice care cen-ters, among others. The school also sent student groups on "justice education trips" to Guatemala, Mexico, Costa Rica, and El Salvador, trips paid for by the students. I heard from students and others in-volved in their lives that these experiences were the highlight of their time in high school and further influenced their career choices.

Even so, the influence of service learning on White students' attitudes toward people of color is mixed (Mitchell, 2008). "Service learning" opportunities like those listed tend to be more available to students and schools with financial resources, both because the school must be able to support local daytrips and because students must pay for extended travel costs. At St Ann's, most of those engag-ing in service work were White, while most of the recipients were people of color. It was entirely possible for a student to commute to St Ann's affluent White neighborhood, only to return with their classmates to their home neighborhood to provide service to their neighbors. While it is possible for White students to encounter racial difference in thought-provoking ways, the structural relationship inhibits change. Ben articulated this tension in his initial interview, where he shared his deeply ambivalent feelings about volunteering at a drop-in shelter:

Kevin: So that's a moment where you feel like the shame is that you can leave, you're visiting in this place where people are struggling and then you kinda go home?

Ben: And how I can sort of derive a positive experience or like I'm supposed to be deriving some sort of positive experience

> from their pain. . . . And I was talking with some people
> about that—how we can sort of have this, we're spending
> thousands of dollars to have this sort of positive experience
> to sort of benefit off these people's pain, or not—I shouldn't
> even say pain. These people's disadvantaged lifestyle. . . . Like
> on one hand I kind of want to go out, experience the world
> and learn about these people, like gather insight like I did
> when I read *The Bluest Eye*, but on the other hand doing so
> kind of, [pause] I dunno, doesn't it make it any better. No,
> the act of gathering insight doesn't make it better. It kind of
> actually makes it a little worse. It's kind of dancing on the
> ashes a little bit.

Ben is sensitive to multiple problematic dynamics at work in this service learning structure, including the power he wields to name others' experience for them as painful, and that "the act of gathering insight" in this way can be exploitative and problematic. Yet he is caught in the relationship available to him, where his assigned role (often literally) is to "learn about these people." The assumption undergirding that task is that by learning more, Ben will experience and be changed by empathy.

When done well, as St Ann's often did, the change will be supported by research and action plans where Ben will be called on, motivated by empathy, to apply his knowledge and privilege to help those he encountered. But even this can be deeply problematic. Ben notices and is troubled by the exploitative quality of "spending thousands of dollars to have this sort of positive experience" with the same emotional investment as reading a book, even if those encounters are pedagogically supported. Even with the contextualizing support he likely received from his teachers, he remains uncomfortable with the exchange. Without the right kind of introspection, the underlying relationship protects or insulates students of privilege from encountering *themselves*, and without that encounter, the exploitative relationship is sustained.

I believe the empathetic relationship Boler describes is at work not only throughout education but in any colonial culture at large, which I believe is demonstrated in the popularity of "White savior" books and movies.[4] Moreover, Boler argues that without fundamentally reorienting the relationship between the people of privilege and the Others they encounter, no amount of framing or sensitivity work can ameliorate the exploitative relationship.

Even before hearing from Ben, I saw this dynamic play out in my school community in several ways. For example, I was tasked with supervising a junior class meeting, which included a presentation from three White juniors who had learned about the struggles of a reservation in the area. Without much preamble, they asked their classmates to collect and donate toiletries to benefit this community of Indigenous folks, then passed the mic to the next speaker. I was floored, aghast in ways I struggled to articulate until I read Boler. What caught me in the moment was how matter of course the ask was. The three students did not provide any context for their request, yet seemingly everyone in the room understood their role as potential benefactor. They were already positioned as givers, whether they chose to or not (and, in all likelihood, few did). There was no discussion about *why* this community was struggling; that they were Indigenous was enough to position them as needy against this mostly White, mostly privileged group. The Whiteness of the speakers and students listening alongside the Indigeneity of those in need can only remain unspoken in a colonial context, where the genocidal history at the root of this difference remains obscured by the very relationship sustained by the request for toiletries. These White students and the Indigenous people they might support were *always already in relationship* through their shared colonial history. Yet "passive empathy" permitted the White students to pretend that they could *choose* to enter a relationship with those in need as potential benefactors or choose to remain innocently disconnected. To be clearly implicated in systems of oppression is to be clearly empowered to change those systems. Without that implication, we risk asking young White people to take up a personal antiracism that is virtually impossible for them to see.

This moment was years ago, long before this project, and it's entirely possible that these students *had* worked through this relationship as part of their research. I believe that their request for toiletries was well intentioned, and I believe that good intentions have sustained White supremacy since its inception. While schooling is permitted or even encouraged to foster this charitable quality in young people, a critical examination of the need for the charity and the source of the generosity is often condemned as political or even anti-American. I've faced such charges myself.

To recognize ourselves as White people who have already benefited at the expense of racial Others is central to the shameful legacy of Whiteness and can be difficult to face, to say the least.

For all of my distaste at these students' presentation, my own classroom followed the same structure for years. My unit on race meant reading *Native Son* (Wright, 2005) alongside the first chapter of Freire's (2007) *Pedagogy of the Oppressed* and asking students to contend with Bigger Thomas's harsh reality in its oppressive context. I hoped the intensity and violence of the story would force students to confront this soberly, or that Jan Erlone, the narrative's well-intentioned but ignorant White character, might reflect to them their own good though inadequate intentions. Our conversations often looked like tense exchanges among my White students and me, all of us caught up in our own anxiety. I hoped for a dialogic classroom where they might encounter antiracist opinions and witness racism through the text in transformative ways. This pedagogy "worked" in the limited ways explored in this project and can benefit from new perspectives.

HOW THIS HELPS

To begin, I return to Boler's (1999) critique of the assumption that empathy leads to action, and her call for testimonial reading and listening, conveniently addressed to *Native Son*. She argues that the insight we are to draw from Bigger's story is not from him, or even from what we feel, but from the ideologies underpinning those feelings:

> To experience rage and shame on Bigger Thomas's behalf is not sufficient; nor is it sufficient to see racism as a "stain" and "infection that prevents a common humanity." Recognizing my position as "judge" granted through the reading privilege, I must learn to question the genealogy of any particular emotional response: My scorn, my evaluation of others' behavior as good or bad, my irritation—each provides a site for interrogation of how the text challenges my investments in familiar cultural values. As I examine the history of a particular emotion, I can identify the taken-for-granted social values and structures of my own historical moment which mirror those encountered by the protagonist. Testimonial reading pushes us to recognize that a novel or biography reflects not merely a distant other, but analogous social relations in our own environment, in which our economic and social positions are implicated. (p. 170, internal citations omitted)

Boler's critique undermines the presumption that *feeling bad* about racism is the same as antiracism while maintaining the essential role played by emotion in challenging social constructs like race. Rather, she suggests turning inward and finding, as suggested by Menakem (2017), Manne (2018), and others, a kind of personal imprint of social values. By examining "the history of a particular emotion," a reader can come to recognize the protagonist not as a version of themself with whom they can empathize, but as a person *already in relationship with* and *subject to* the reader's beliefs and behaviors in their world. In other words, passive empathy permits a "safe" and ultimately facile encounter, where I as a reader can *feel alongside* a protagonist without any personal implication. By looking more closely at those feelings, a reader can come to understand and critique the social values they unwittingly carry with them to the text. This social- and self-directed critique opens new and generative possibilities for the reader, who comes to understand the ways they are *always already in relationship with* (through colonialism, capitalism, Whiteness, etc.) those they encounter in texts.

In summary, Boler argues that empathetic catharsis, such as the experience of reading about the comeuppance of a White racist at the hands of a Black protagonist, precludes action. Because that catharsis dismisses differences in the name of sameness, that which constitutes a challenge to the notion of innocence or goodness within the empathetic self becomes subsumed into the self through an empathy that values sameness over suffering. Here, suffering is not *shared with* so much as *utilized by* the listener, who, in this role, could be called a bystander or spectator. As Boler argues, others' suffering serves as a socioemotional voyeuristic experience for the listener, who has no relationship with or obligation to the suffering. Like a fear experience inside of a carnival's haunted house, the feelings are simultaneously real and meaningless.

Boler suggests that in order for empathy to generate change, it must hail the listener in such a way that the listener joins with the story and experiences its discomfort; what she calls "A Pedagogy of Discomfort." Zembylas (2006) describes this as testimonial listening or witnessing. Witnessing can be painful as it challenges the worldview of the witness, bringing them face to face with "some massive and previously unthinkable disaster or victimization," which "shatters one's worldview" (Zembylas, 2006, p. 314). Unlike the cathartic fear experienced in a haunted house, witnessing demands that the witness reckon with their role in a world that permits such violence to happen.[5] The function of witnessing is to destabilize the witness in "a fundamentally powerful affective experience; affects operate on both the psychic and social level by challenging one's agency to imagine oneself as an ethical and political actor" (Zembylas, 2006, p. 314). This reckoning demands that the witness either take up action against the violence or relinquish their belief in themselves as "ethical and political actors."

A Pedagogy of Discomfort therefore poses risks. "Such work [of pursuing justice] not only draws us closer to the suffering, *it makes us suffer*" (Hook & West, as quoted in Zembylas & Chubbuck, 2008, p. 164, emphasis added). Zembylas (2006) adds that a "crisis is essential in order for bearing witness to occur" (p. 320).[6] Boler's Pedagogies of Discomfort have been taken up by several scholars concerned with how discomfort can be achieved generatively and ethically (Chubbuck & Zembylas, 2008; Leonardo & Zembylas, 2013). Each of these caution that the affective work of pedagogies of discomfort is fraught, "risks inflicting violence" (Zembylas 2015), and could lead to a hopeless despair.

Even so, Boler argues that empathy must hail the listener in such a way that the listener joins with the story and experiences its discomfort. This leads to what Dominick LaCapra calls "empathetic unsettlement," where the student "reactivate[s] and transmit[s] not trauma but an unsettlement that manifests empathy (but not full identification) with the victim" (as quoted in Zembylas, 2006, p. 321). This unsettlement is a generative space wherein young White people can encounter not only the stories and lives of those who experience racism, but themselves. I explore the new pedagogies of empathy, including pedagogies of discomfort, in more detail in Chapter 7.

CONCLUSION

In the previous chapters I focused on how White privilege pedagogy can seek to disarm students without fully understanding what in them feels vulnerable and in need of defense, sometimes leaving them bound and hopeless. Asking that White students confess to being racist or exposing them to racism without adequate support has not led young White people to take up antiracism as intended. I used to believe that, armed with the right set of arguments, I could convince my White students of racism, as though Whiteness and White identity rests on logic and reason, as though the entire history of Whiteness is a manifestation of logic and reason rather than a panicked denial and desperate need for acceptance. Rather, if Whiteness is at its heart a set of emotional maneuvers, then White resistance to antiracism is also a set of emotional maneuvers, itself in part a reaction to protect a vulnerable self. Attempting to force students to recognize the reality of racism as we see it, as White privilege pedagogy suggests, fails to recognize these contexts and can pose unnecessary risks. As Zembylas (2013) argues,

> Critical pedagogues need to be more critically aware of the emotional consequences when they categorize individuals into "oppressors" and "oppressed"; failing to understand how students' emotional attachments are strongly entangled with traumatic historical circumstances and material conditions will undermine teachers' pedagogical interventions. (pp. 179–180)

By avoiding these divides, classroom conversations about race can be reframed as working alongside resistant students, rather than working against them. Antiracist work can benefit from trauma-aware classrooms as well as the introspection and self-awareness that comes from his work. Menakem's (2017) work with racial trauma is useful here, as is van der Kolk's (2015), whose book on trauma concludes with the poet Auden: "Truth, like love and sleep, resents / approaches that are too intense" (p. 127). I believe this can be a helpful reminder when addressing race.

As demonstrated in this work, our students are likely more aware of these shortcomings and more prepared for more effective methods than we imagine. Ben saw through and was critical of service projects that assumed his encounter with racial others could be an uncomplicated "learning experience." Even participants sympathetic to the antiracist project of our clumsy pedagogies of discomfort, like Maria or Ali, took these up uneasily. This is to say that our own unease with these pedagogies, as well as those of our students, are well-founded. While we are in need of new perspectives and ways of getting unstuck, we have not been hopelessly lost in the dark. The following and final chapter spends time with ways of getting unstuck.

CHAPTER 7

Getting Unstuck

The Dreamers will have to learn to struggle themselves, to understand
that the field for the Dream, the stage where they have painted themselves
white, is the deathbed of us all.

—Ta-Nehisi Coates

I began this book in my classroom, where I struggled with the anti-racist pedagogies I had inherited. With the help of the untold histories, insights, and critiques of Whiteness from Chapter 2, I spent 5 months with 10 courageous young people exploring race; I am deeply in their debt. I cannot overstate how much I learned from the participants' vulnerability, insights, humor, and compassion. If I've grown any smarter about Whiteness, that gain is thanks in large part to their work. In Chapter 3 the participants and I worked through how they could or could not talk about race, as well as the origins and sustainers of those constrained discourses. I considered the depressive effects of these discourses, especially calling out, in Chapter 4. Chapter 5 then took up the role of emotion in how these young White people did and did not take up White privilege pedagogy and antiracism, including how they became bound within those discourses. Chapter 6 explored these emotional processes in more detail, focusing on shame, trauma, and empathy.

Here, I conclude with a consideration of how we might shift away from bounded racial discourses to more generative positions. It is my hope that White people may no longer feel overwhelmed or complacent about White supremacy, but that we can recognize and address it with some clarity and conviction. As I explore next, I believe we are closer to meaningful antiracism than we seem to think we are.

We know that the ways we've been taught to make sense of race, racism, and Whiteness are deeply flawed and inhibit our antiracist possibilities. We are rightly cautioned, once again, by Charles Mills's (1997) Racial Contract as well as enormously helpful texts like *Despite* the *Best Intentions* (Lewis & Diamond, 2015) and podcasts like *The New York Times' Nice White Parents* (Joffe-Walt, 2020), that much of the ways we've come to understand race and Whiteness is not only mis-informed, but counterproductive. For example, we know that White supremacists are not only gaining political and social legitimacy, but that they have become versed in the discourses of the left, claiming victimhood in the same ways and sometimes using the same language as marginalized groups. We need to shift our strategies.

I believe we can, broadly speaking, make sense of antiracism for White people as having three parts. The first follows Guinier's (2004) proposal of a "paradigm shift from racial liberalism to racial literacy" (p. 100), in hopes of providing counternarratives to official antiracisms like multiculturalism. I've worked to provide such counternarratives in the histories told in Chapter 2 as well as pursuing the critiques raised by the young White people in Chapters 3–5. Additionally, we know that commonly used antiracist discourses such as WPP have largely failed to move young White people to antiracist action, instead often binding them through White shame. I believe this is, in part, because WPP severely limits ways of making sense of that privilege, leaving White people with few options other than to feel bad or reject the idea entirely. While antiracism is not only about White privilege, I believe making sense of privilege can be an important starting place when undertaking antiracism.

Working through my privileges requires that I uncover and exam-ine the sometimes painful aspects of myself submerged by Whiteness. Chapters 5 and 6 sought to frame this internal work in the contexts of shame, trauma, and empathy, which are central to the self-work I consider the second stage in the journey of antiracism. I visualize the first stage as reimagining the structures of Whiteness and our White supremacist country, while the second stage brings those new ways of understanding Whiteness to bear on myself as a White person. With new perspectives afforded by more clear-eyed understandings of the histories and social structures of White Americans, I become better equipped to witness and dismantle my internalized Whiteness. Again, I propose to begin that excavation through new ways of understand-ing shame, trauma, and empathy.

The third stage of this journey is undertaking antiracist action in the world. In my pursuit of efficiency and impact, I find myself want-ing to begin here at the expense of the personal work. Of course, these stages constitute false boundaries and are always undertaken concurrently. I name them as three in order to highlight the need for the first two. Without a more powerful and accurate analysis of race and Whiteness, and without ongoing personal work, antiracist action risks perpetuating the structures it seeks to oppose.[1] Further, while we will always benefit from a community of support and consultation, the less work White people do on the first two stages, the more dependent they will be on others to guide them in the third, and the less powerful their action will tend to be. Antiracist work is personal, contextual, and as Menakem argues, emergent: as we work through our histories and ourselves, the work in front of us, the changes to our curriculum and lives, become apparent.

This chapter explores the emotional paralysis generated by guilt and shame-driven pedagogies of privilege, how neoliberal norms of logic and reasoning forbid necessary emotional processing, and how attempts to generate empathy can create a kind of trauma in White people repeatedly exposed to horrific racial violence without pedagogical or emotional support. I call for a shift in how race work is undertaken in the classroom, noting that much of the critiqued ideology of our contemporary race talk, including listening to the stories of racial Others, feeling on behalf of racial Others, and an ideology of hope, all continue to play a meaningful role. I begin with White privilege.

REVISITING WHITE PRIVILEGE

My personal Whiteness work, contending with my social and financial privileges, has involved making sense of what has stood in the way of my antiracist practice. Yet the interrogation often leaves me, like Heidi, Ali, and Ben, feeling shameful and stuck; "What took me so long? How have I tolerated my complicity in White supremacy? What allowed me to carry on day by day while I benefited from the injustices survived by people of color? What is wrong with me?" Making sense of my White privilege, undeniably central to my experience of being White in the United States, has been constrained by the available models. In a way, by not prescribing what one should do with this privilege, White privilege pedagogy encourages this dead end. Should one apply their privileges outwardly, or seek to abdicate them entirely? White folks are left to work these problems out on their own, so that "commonsense" White ways of being drive the problematic and incomplete ways privilege gets taken up. A broader consideration of White privilege can afford broader antiracist possibilities. I believe WPP fails to take seriously the privileges it addresses, and that taking them more seriously might afford White people more antiracist possibilities. I suggest we make three changes to our sense of antiracism.

First, I have understood my antiracism as a White person, like multiculturalism, like affirmative action, as outward facing, so that I can "give back" out of my privilege to those who have less. As a person of privilege, I am supposed to give of that privilege to those who have been harmed by the systemic oppression from which I have benefited, a kind of effort to right a wrong. The problem WPP presumes is that others have *less*, not that I have *more*, and so long as we are all convinced to acquire more, few of us will believe we ever have *enough*. There is no "giving" our way out of this dynamic, and perhaps an innate sense of that informs some of the resistance to ideas like reparations. The fatal flaw of WPP is that it remains rooted in neoliberal individualism—that I must give of mine—rather than orienting toward collective action. Antiracism is not individual work and cannot be individually oriented.

Written out, the problematic White savior dynamic inherent to giving of my privilege becomes clear, and I feel the discomfort Ben articulated in the previous chapter. Not only does this model depend on my willingness to help, but it stubbornly locates the problem of White supremacy within those who survive it rather than those who profit by it. Again, it is a problem of having less. So long as I can comfortably locate the problems of White supremacy in unsafe neighborhoods and underfunded schools across town, I can comfortably avoid my complicity in those problems and imagine myself as a savior opting in to racial justice. This is the myth of official antiracisms that serve to uphold White supremacy in the guise of liberal action.

In countless conversations with well-intentioned White people, as well as within my own thinking, the ultimate destination of WPP is that I give up my accrued wealth, sell my nice house, move into one of those neighborhoods across town, and send my kids to one of those underfunded schools. This is as unsatisfying as it is unrealistic and imagines a highly limited impact of my antiracism. Who is changed if I move across town, or give up my financial security? What is the extent of my impact? What systems are changed? When it comes to wealth and opportunity hoarding, antiracism is not about redistributing individual wealth but working to reduce the need for individualized wealth.

There are, however, three aspects of White privilege that can and must be simply and powerfully redistributed at an individual level: time, attention, and energy. I've only recently come to understand the ways I accumulate time, attention, and energy at the direct expense of others onto whom I outsource the mental and physical labor of things like picking up groceries or making dinner. Moreover, the labor struggles within companies like Amazon and Uber give the lie to the myth of the gig economy wherein I create jobs by having my lunch delivered to my home. As I participate in those systems of late capitalism, I extract time, attention, and energy in the same way I extract money by investing in the stock market. In the same way it's cheaper to be rich, it also takes less time and effort. In addition to shopping local, and patronizing minority- and women-owned businesses, I can apply that time, attention, and energy to the causes of racial justice rather than expanding my leisure or, more likely, my professional ambitions.

Second, my White privileges do more than cushion my bank account and insulate me from police molestation. They provide a safe and comfortable bed on which I can close my eyes and sleep. My privileges are the car window between me and the person asking for money on the exit ramp. His naked need is made more tolerable by the window. Like that window, my privileges deaden my consciousness to the workings of Whiteness. In a way, that is their role; it's why they exist. Recall the origins of Whiteness, where those in power literally redistributed wealth from African laborers to European laborers and told those Europeans that their superior Whiteness explained the subsequent wealth gap. The privileges of Whiteness and the mythology of the American Dream and the very real access it affords suggest to White people that they are in control, that they can protect themselves and their loved ones from the world where others suffer. It suggests this to White people by convincing them that they are *different* than those who suffer.

I believe that Whiteness, at its core, suggests to White people that they are safe *because* others are not. This can be seen in the justifications Whiteness offers for the appalling racial disparities in state-sanctioned education, violence, and wealth. White people are meant to be comforted by diminishing the severity of police brutality; to admit otherwise is to recognize our own vulnerability to police violence, to challenge our sense of safety and security in the world, and to admit our complicity in such violence. Why else would White people deny the evidence of their own eyes? The White privilege to be free from police harassment permits our ignorance of that privilege as well as our comfort in having it. Similarly, White people are comforted by blaming those with less for their financial situation. Whiteness tells us that, in Freire's (2007) words, we have more because of our effort, our "courage to take risks. If others do not have more, it is because they are incompetent and lazy" (p. 59). In a racially inequitable society, White people "having more" is an injustice, and is only acceptable with such evasions and justifications.

The White invulnerability to state harassment or financial struggles or lower-class status that come with Whiteness are all invulnerabilities by comparison. To suggest invulnerability by comparison is a central role of Whiteness and White supremacy. Yet the relative (and false) invulnerability offered by Whiteness, what I believe is an underexamined aspect of White supremacy, is itself a false prize not worth its terrible cost. Our vulnerability is so central to our humanity that to lose it is to lose touch with ourselves. Without vulnerability, life loses its immediacy and value. I wonder if it is precisely the loss of this vulnerability and happiness that leaves us bereft and drives our ongoing investment in the noxious comforts of Whiteness. In other words, like Ouroboros, the snake that eats its own tail, White privileges offer a salve for the wounds inflicted by acquiring and having White privileges. In a way, I have struggled so hard to keep these privileges (or, indeed, to give them up!) that I failed to recognize the humanity I had already lost.

Finally, in addition to providing the false comfort and sense of invulnerability, White privileges are sustained by a distorted White reality, Mills's (1997) Racial Contract and May's (2015) "agreement to know the world wrongly" (p. 190). Without a racialized moral psychology that masks the workings of Whiteness, the injustices intrinsic to Whiteness become visible and intolerable. Of course, these injustices are always plainly visible to people of color and emergently visible to White people undertaking their emancipation from White supremacy. Despite these obfuscations, we can recognize glimpses of the truth. For example, the truth is sometimes perversely manifested in justifications of inequality, such as when the wealthy celebrate the simple happiness of the poor. When the privileged profess an admiration (and jealousy that something so wonderful is not theirs) of this happiness, they betray an unacknowledged loss and longing. For me, making better sense of why I have remained beholden to my privileges helps me move beyond them. Moreover, as Menakem (2017) argues, as I come to recognize the workings of Whiteness in my life, my antiracist possibilities emerge.

In other words, this second stage of my antiracist practice is not so much about the lives of racial Others, or even my White thoughts about racial Others, but my White thoughts about my White self and my White world. Toni Morrison (1991) reminds us that "the subject of the dream is the dreamer" (p. 17), that my thoughts and feelings toward racial Others are always informed by my understanding of myself. Therefore, my antiracist sense-making begins with me and the dream that has kept me comfortably ensconced within my Whiteness and privilege. Waking from the dream that distances me from my problems won't be easy, but, if you are reading this book, I imagine you are convinced of the greater cost of staying asleep.

NEW PEDAGOGIES OF PRIVILEGE: SOLIDARITY

The cost of Whiteness to White people is the fullness of their humanity. White people are not whole because of the trauma of becoming White, and that brokenness binds us to our privileges. As Tanner (2018) writes, "Yes, whiteness privileges white people in the United States. But it might devastate them too" (p. 141). This is not a simple weight. If White people are to claim their goodness as White people (and I believe we should), we must recognize the immense, life-threatening power of Whiteness that has kept White people in thrall to White supremacy for generations. White people must acknowledge and move beyond the strain under which we have lived that has bound us to our Whiteness, to our sense of moving through the world with nothing but our own know-how and effort. Education offers several helpful possibilities.

In addition to orienting ourselves toward collective action, human vulnerability, and the critical thinking necessary to counter dominant and misguided ways of being, we can foster a critical awareness of the default ways we think and talk about race. As problematic as it is, I believe WPP is always operant in conversations about race; we cannot avoid it or pretend that it does not influence our thinking. Instead, we can make visible the ways WPP has been helpful and unhelpful, and we can complicate the notion of privilege in the process.

First, we must push against the belief that financial wealth and social status are the only metrics of human value. It feels a little on the nose to articulate that, but reorienting the ways we value human life is fundamental to antiracism. WPP importantly recognized and popularized the ways Whiteness advantages White people, yet it did not complicate those privileges and never intended to explore the ways Whiteness, in Tanner's words, "might devastate them too." Moreover, White privilege assumes a deficit model of people of color, that BIPoC folks *have less*, without complicating what exactly they have less *of*, and does not recognize the many important ways that BIPoC folks *have*, even in a system in which they are systematically disadvantaged. In other words, there are ways of being that do not rely on accumulation at all, and moving away from White ways of being might involve counterintuitive strategies.

As one example, Lewis and Diamond (2015) argue that any time we enforce the rules with discretion, we risk acting out our self-interest and internalized biases. They provide ample evidence of this. They suggest that the solution to inequitably applied discipline policies is to apply them assiduously, rather than applying them with more leniency. Then, if the even application of rules results in the over-punishment of resourced students, those students' families will insist that the rules change. This removes the impact of privilege by removing the need for privileges—as in, the answer to the problem of White privilege is not that everyone has more, but that everyone *needs* less.

Further, however obvious it might feel to name that wealth is not the only measure of human life, within a capitalist society it remains a powerful and revolutionary sentiment. Therefore, any conversation about privilege benefits from complicating those privileges. How else can we value human life? What if our problem wasn't scarcity, as capitalism suggests, but notions of happiness and connection, and other things that grow when given away? What if the solution to White supremacy was collective and structural change rather than individual action? How can we rearrange schooling to celebrate collectivity in addition to (or in lieu of!) individual academic accomplishments? And, cautioned that Whiteness also protects White people from stressors, in what ways does Whiteness get in the way of the happiness of White people? Based on their skepticism of WPP, the benefits of their own Whiteness, and schooling in general, I suggest that young White people are primed for this conversation and can be helpful guides as we reimagine antiracist education.

Second, recognizing the work my White privilege does to insulate me from the ways I am implicated in Whiteness, I must ask what else insulates me. For myself, I benefit from recognizing the ways that knowing and needing to know more, the spaces where I am comfortable, insulated me against feeling. As a teacher, a scholar, and product of our education system, I am at particular risk of withdrawing into my brain. Moreover, Whiteness, masculinity, and Western ways of being all reinforce a mind–body dualism antithetical to antiracism. While I was encouraged to think and know my way out of racism and

White supremacy, Whiteness lived in my body. As Menakem (2017) cautions, "We've tried to teach our brains to think better about race. But white-body supremacy doesn't live in our thinking brains. It lives and breathes in our bodies" (p. 5). There will always be another book to read, another pitfall to learn about and avoid.

Upon reflection, I've come to recognize that learning was a way for me to feel like I was doing something without changing myself. Reading was a way for me to engage with Whiteness while remaining comfortable. Even many of my conversations with my White friends served to reinforce my goodness rather than hold me accountable. I could feel myself wanting to build my knowledge about racism even as I knew plenty. I could always justify learning more, reading more, talking more. Yet for me, knowing more about Whiteness did not automatically translate to action or change, in large part because knowing kept me out of my body. It served to insulated me against feeling, and I could not change while I remained insulated. Further, I learned in part as a way to cope with the pain of systemic racism, and every coping mechanism is a release for the tension that might otherwise push me to change.

Following Menakem (2017) and so many other scholars of color, I believe body work is central to antiracism. When I can permit myself to feel the ways I am harmed by Whiteness, I can become undone and enter a generative discomfort. To surrender not only my White privileges but the Whiteness that keeps me in my head is to confront the ways I am related to those I have ignored and harmed, that my liberation is bound with theirs. In other words, the shift from knowing to feeling is, in part, about empathy.

REVISITING EMPATHY

I recently shared part of my leadership journey for a White affinity group in a teacher workshop series. The workshop used racial affinity groupings to, in part, create space where teachers of color could discuss the challenges of working within the White-dominated field of education—a conversation topic made possible by segregated spaces. Afterward, a colleague who shared her own journey as a Black educator with the affinity group for teachers of color told me that some White participants lamented that they were sad to miss her story. My colleague certainly had a lot to offer professionally, and I understood where those participants were coming from. However, as she described how she told the White teachers that I also had a great deal to offer, I was struck. However great my story was, I could hardly imagine a moment where teachers of color would rather listen to my story as a White educator than the story of another teacher of color. Yet the opposite desire happened all the time; I had felt it myself. Moreover, I'll admit that part of my desire to hear teachers of color talk about race was to "peek behind the curtain," to have access to what is typically inaccessible to me as a White person. I'm reminded of Maria's gratitude at being allowed to listen in while her friends of color shared stories about being BIPoC while they worked in the costume room. This suggests that the conversation was noteworthy in part because her peers of color carried on as if she were one of them and not conspicuously White. Indeed, she is clearly respected and trusted by her peers, and the stories she heard mattered to her a great deal. Yet after that conversation, Maria remained White in a White supremacist world, without any renewed sense of her Whiteness or what she could do about it.

Like White privilege in the context of White supremacy, crossracial empathy presumes a relationship that is, in some ways, antithetical to antiracism. This empathy also, like White privilege, orients White people away from themselves. Boler (1999) offers a critique of the ways White people (or any oppressor) encounter racial Others through a presumption of sameness that fails to consider power relations and leave the oppressive relationship intact, as I explored in Chapter 6. Further, this problematic empathetic relationship operates throughout Whiteness and White ways of being. My desire for access in this example, as a White person, to BIPoC conversations wherein I might figure as an oppressor, however abstractly, are suspect. My access is desirable, in part, because I presume to elide my responsibility as an oppressor. I presume to pretend, however unconsciously, that I am a member of that group, a comrade, shaking my head at Whiteness, without explicitly including myself in that category.

Aligning oneself with the oppressed as an oppressor is an understandable desire, and feeling it should not be condemned. Rather, the feeling represents a laudable longing for comradeship, for interracial solidarity, for the very things we hope for. Yet, following Boler (1999), we must recognize that these feelings are incomplete, in part because empathetic identification is recursive; it imagines one in the others' shoes. As she writes, "The agent of empathy, then, is a fear for oneself" (p. 159). The feelings are also incomplete by denying or ignoring power relations. Passive empathy fails to implicate the reader within the social problem. So long as White people identify with BIPoC folks without being implicated in the racism they experience, and so long as White people believe that race isn't about them, their antiracism will be incomplete. The reader, therefore, is without an analysis that locates them within the problem. They can pretend they are choosing to help out of their own goodness, but without context they are typically at a loss about where to begin and can only empathize (and, as Boler [1999] writes, "these 'others' whose lives we imagine don't want empathy, they want justice" [p. 157]). Like these participants, a White person watching a White savior film, or reading a protest novel, is not shown their complicity.

The empathetic relationship of White savior ideology is underwritten by a short-circuited longing. The reader can experience a superficial solidarity without having done any of the personal work necessary to understand how they contribute to cycles of oppression. The oppression they come to understand exists without context or history or is advanced by cartoonish racists and top-hatted capitalists. While this false solidarity can *feel* deeply and attractively cathartic, the missing complicity is precisely what can inform antiracist and revolutionary action. As Boler (1999) explains, "What is at stake is not only the ability to empathize with the very distant other, but to recognize oneself as implicated in the social forces that create the climate of obstacles the other must confront. . . . I suggest that unlike passive empathy, testimonial reading requires a self-reflective *participation*" (p. 166). In short, Maria's Whiteness, being unremarkable, does not exact a cost nor provide any insight in the interaction. She is neither implicated nor empowered. A revised pedagogy of empathy seeks to do both.

NEW PEDAGOGIES OF EMPATHY: RELATIONAL READING

As I observed in the previous chapter, moving away from passive empathy relies on making sense of our location within oppressive systems rather than as spectator to them. What Boler calls testimonial reading involves reading as if one is encountering a real person rather than a contestable historical account, and that kind of reading requires an introspective vulnerability. As she explains, this reading "involves recognizing moral relations not simply as a "perspectival" difference— "we all see things differently"—but rather, that how we see or choose not to see has ethical implications and may even cause others to suffer" (p. 195). This is a significant change in a reader's role, conventionally understood to be much less personal, along the lines of "code breaker" or posing critical literacy questions about who is and is not represented. Even reader-response criticism orients the reader's experience as between the text and themselves rather than implicating the reader's world in the text. In *Letting Go of Literary Whiteness*, Borsheim-Black and Sarigianedes (2019) call for a "racialized reader response," foregrounding the role of race in literary analysis.

Similarly, Boler (1999) calls for White readers to process not only their interpretations, opinions, or even feelings, but the sociopolitical origins of those feelings:

> The testimonial reader must attend to herself as much as to the other . . . in terms of the affective obstacles that prevent the reader's acute attention to the power relations guiding her responses and judgements. For example, to experience a surge of irritation at the text allows the reader to examine the potential analysis: Does she dismiss the text or protagonist on some count, or examine her own safeguard investment that desires to dismiss the text out of irritation? Might irritation, for example, indicate the reader's desire to avoid confronting the articulated pain? (p. 169)

A reader, therefore, is called on to not only investigate the historicity or perspective of a text but their own emotional response to it. Through this admittedly challenging investigation, their implication in or relationship to the suffering of the characters in the text become visible within their emotional response.

I'm reminded of a pivotal moment in Lee Man Wah's 1994 film *The Color of Fear*, when David, who is White, comes to recognize the truth of the racisms faced by Victor and other men of color in the group. Mun Wah pushes David to examine his resistance:

Lee Mun Wah: So what's keeping you from believing that that's happening to Victor? Just believing, not to know why that's happening to him. But what's keeping you from believing that that's happening—

David: Because it seems like such a harsh life. *And I just don't want to believe*—I would assume, Victor, that your life is really that hard, difficult, and unpleasant.

Lee Mun Wah: What would it mean, David, then, if the life really was that harsh? What would that mean in your life, if it really was that harsh for—?

David: Well, it would be a travesty of life. (emphasis added)

David's resistance is not rooted in a stubborn belief in White racial superiority, or in his attachment to his position of privilege as a White man in the conventional sense. Rather, David is inhibited by his attachment to a worldview wherein people are, in general, treated fairly. Mun Wah had to redirect David to his resistances, and we can do the same with ourselves and our White students. In order for David to make sense of Victor's experience, he must reconsider his place in the world, his understanding of how the world operates, and himself. This reconsideration is not possible within a single conversation or unit. Nor is it possible within a one-off training or workshop.

Reorienting from consumption to relationship is a significant shift in classrooms oriented around lecture and material presentation, yet the move is consistent with our educational goals. Not only does working toward relational reading better position our students to become change makers, but the fundamental shift of Boler's pedagogy of discomfort brings the students into direct relationship with our curricula. As educators, we are still working to help our students locate themselves in the text; we are now doing so without subsuming meaningful cultural differences with a placid (and, I would add, less interesting) sameness.

Boler suggests that students (and teachers) undertake this work collectively, perhaps as part of the project of making sense of a text. In addition to tasks of critical literacy, working to locate the readers, however hypothetically, within the text can become part of the habit of reading. Importantly, this task of reading against the grain of the text must be undertaken with eyes open. When reading about slavery, my bias will be to identify with heroic figures rather than the more ordinary bystanders—northern merchants and wage laborers, for example. Recalling the category of nonracist between racist and antiracist, the broad category into which nearly all White people fall, is helpful here. Conversations about race in the United States benefit from working through King's (2018) "white moderate who is more devoted to 'order' than to justice; who prefers a negative peace which is the absence of tension to a positive peace which is the presence of justice" (p. 12), rather than (or at least in addition to) learning about Harriet Tubman's astonishing heroism. The goal of such a pedagogy is a deeper understanding of the Other through a fuller (and more critical) understanding of oneself. "In a sense, the reader is called upon to meet the text with her own testimony, rather than using the other as a catalyst or a substitute for oneself" (Boler, 1999, p. 172). A group of young people working through their testimony, through their place in their own historical moment, is fostering the extraordinary potential to develop a clear perspective of themselves, empowering them to seize that moment for change. Once again, their empowerment comes from their implication in their moment.

This deeply personal and challenging work can be bolstered by recognizing what we, as White people, stand to gain. On this, Boler (and I) defer to Minnie Bruce Pratt's must-read essay "Identity: Skin/Blood/Heart." Pratt identifies three gains, the first of which is worth quoting at length:

> I learn a way of looking at the world that is more accurate, complex, multi-layered, multi-dimensioned, more truthful. . . . I gain truth when I expand my constricted eye, an eye that has only let in what I have been taught to see. But there have been other constrictions around my heart . . . kin to a terror that has been in my birth culture for years, for centuries: the terror of a people who have set themselves apart and above, who have wronged others, and feel they are about to be found out and punished. (Pratt, 1984, pp. 6–7)

The second is the possibility of living into a vulnerability that lies beyond that fear, and the third "is the relief afforded through the opportunity to move beyond the pain inherent to 'separation,' and distance from others" (p. 182). In other words, White people stand to grow by reengaging with their surrendered humanity. Again, I am reminded of the lifelong aspect to this work, and that writing out those potential gains in a sentence is reductive and glib. Perhaps more importantly, I must remain mindful that the structures I have internalized, however comfortable, are deeply flawed, and that however challenging or threatening the change, new ways of being offer a healthier and more wholesome existence.

These are self-oriented benefits of antiracism, which, even as we recognize that White people must change, can make White people uncomfortable. The young White people I worked with blanched at the prospect that they might gain anything from tackling racism; the thought struck them as almost treacherous. I believe this discomfort is rooted in a zero-sum possessive consciousness, where White people believe they are meant to have less while BIPoC have more, or that racial equity means that White people ought to be subjected to the violences of White supremacy for a while to somehow even things out. In short, as Pratt said, we are problematically oriented to antiracism by the fear that White people "are about to be found out and punished." That White people are conditioned by these fears in order to avoid cross-racial solidarity does not lessen them, but it might motivate us to move beyond them. Rather than fearing for my physical safety, how can I embrace the fears attendant to the vulnerability of making mistakes, or of not knowing the right thing to do or say? "Pratt emphasizes how what we learn *not* to see is shaped by fear, and how learning to see differently requires a willingness to live with new fears" (Boler, 1999, p. 182, emphasis in original).

As with the rest of this work, it is important to take seriously these new fears. Rather than fearing the Other, White people might fear changing our understanding of our place in our world. Rather than fearing our physical vulnerability, we might fear being emotionally vulnerable to our complicity in racial oppression. In a sense, we are inviting White students to confront suppressed and/or ignored realities that can feel threatening for these reasons. As Boler says,

> There is every temptation to turn our backs, to maintain the habit of denial, and to keep secrets from ourselves through the numb consumption of another's suffering, grateful for distances that seems to confirm our safety. Yet, at best, this illusion of safety and distance in which most live is precarious.[2] (p. 172)

White people have existed behind this denial for centuries. Moreover, that denial, sustained by the numb consumption of others' suffering, wounds White people deeply. Like our privileges, passive empathy falsely suggests a window between us and oppression, behind which we can remain innocent to the world, a screen through which we can passively observe violences and pretend they happen to benefit or protect someone else rather than ourselves.

Our work is not only to extend outrage on behalf of those we do not know, but to recognize that even before we encounter the Other through a book or movie or service project, we are always already in relationship. Our participation in the social systems that oppress Others implicates us in their suffering. Making sense of our implication (and only making sense of our implication) empowers us to transform our role in oppressive social systems.

There's a healthier world waiting to replace our flawed White one. We can and must reorient ourselves to this. The further White people get from the familiar Whiteness, the closer we get to solidarity and authenticity. This is antiracism: attainment not abdication, growth not loss, wholeness not brokenness. Revised pedagogies must reclaim the value of feeling sadness and experiencing vulnerability in order for White people to become whole. And of course, eliciting such personal responses must be done with care and compassion. While distinct from theories of passive empathy, strategic empathy is one such elicitation.

STRATEGIC EMPATHY

In her work with emotion and economic class, Lindquist (2004) describes what she calls strategic empathy:

> What made this strategy work, I think, was my willingness to make myself strategically naïve in two moments: first, in seeking advice about how we should conduct discussions . . . and then later, when (working hard against my own emotional need to negatively evaluate some of the perspectives I was hearing about the war) I worked to communicate empathy for their positions *as affective responses*. (pp. 203–204, emphasis in original)

I and many other teachers have used her first step, opening the ground rules governing class conversations, in order to help generate ownership and participation. Yet I have resisted her second moment of naiveté where she affects empathy for their potentially harmful positions. For one, I am responsible for the discourse of my classroom, and I worry that I might provide sanction to unchallenged remarks.

I believe I was mistaken in two related ways: I was overestimating my own importance as arbiter, and I was treating the learning space as *mine* rather than as collaborative. To be sure, shifting toward a collaborative learning space takes time and effort, as teacher-centric classrooms remain the default setting for most students. Developing student- or project-centric classroom work fosters an environment where teachers have the flexibility to serve as guide, permitting students to flesh out racial misconceptions with less risk of those views metastasizing, provided they are able to do that in racially homogenous groups. Strategic empathy is the pedagogical tool that gives teachers discursive access to both these spaces and resistant students.

Second, it is possible to be affectively empathetic toward a perspective without affirming it. Repeating or rephrasing what someone is saying and mirroring their affect is a powerful way to listen—I do this with my own young children all the time—and does not suggest agreement. Further, my students are always well aware of my bias toward justice, which might help clarify the extent of my empathy. By mirroring students' affect and sentiment, including validating shared sentiments such as the importance of fairness and equality and the difficulty of dealing with racism as White people, teachers can help White students process their resistance to antiracism in helpful ways. Yes, fairness is important. Why does antiracism seem unfair? I also value equality. What's the difference between equality and equity? I believe that your ancestors made sacrifices, worked hard, and suffered; mine did too. That's real. How was Whiteness at work in those histories?

Perhaps more importantly, attempting to *convince* someone of racism or any other emotionally held belief simply doesn't work, as anyone who has tried can attest.[3] In my work I had the opportunity to ask David, a participant whose views on race had shifted, what had changed him: "A huge thing that really changed me was, it was not really finding new perspectives, but it was seeing how wrong a lot of this stuff I believed was. So it really wasn't that I was pushed anywhere." This suggests that antiracist pedagogy is better served by finding ways to draw out student's racist beliefs through strategic empathy in hopes that these misinformed views wither under scrutiny. This poses very real risks to other students. Simply hearing harmful dominant ideologies, for example a justification of slavery or so-called "positive stereotypes" of racial groups, can be harmful.

Strategic empathy problematically raises the risk of potential harm to BIPoC in these conversations when we ask them to tolerate, even for a short time, hurtful ideologies. I always prioritize the well-being of marginalized groups in those contexts, at the "expense" of being strategically empathetic to racist, Islamophobic, sexist, homophobic, xenophobic, and other harmful views. I cannot abide socioemotional growth at the expense of someone else's emotional well-being, however temporarily. We must not educate the oppressors on the backs of the oppressed. I also believe that processing toxic ideologies requires airing them while mitigating as much risk as possible. These conflicting needs call for racial affinity groups, and I'm not sure what to do with that in my racially integrated classroom. I have no simple answer. Our work here must be as sensitive as any other classroom work regarding race. The work of racial justice calls for community-wide intervention, potentially allowing for racial affinity groupings. Strategic empathy offers the possibilities of carefully pushing through unwelcome perspectives.

RADICAL HOPE

The second concept, in a way, addresses this tension. In his exploration of White emotion and affect, Zembylas (2014) is concerned about how difficult knowledge can be productively addressed. He recognized that empathetic encounters with difficult knowledge are moments of crisis, and that students encountering difficult knowledge can fall into despair, not unlike the boundedness described by participants, and not unlike the despair we might feel after a lengthy encounter with race. Zembylas (2014) cites Britzman's work on the possibilities of hope within pedagogical encounters with trauma: "How can the curriculum be organized, she asks, in a way that does not provide closure but rather the possibilities to repair traumatic experiences" (p. 394). This is the very problem confronting classroom teachers as we work to shift our antiracist pedagogies away from despair and boundedness and toward what Farley (2009) calls radical hope.

Farley, a history scholar, is addressing the crisis faced by the educators of children confronted with difficult historical knowledge, such as slavery or Jim Crow. These educators typically move to protect the innocence of the child, yet Farley (2009) points out that "no matter how meticulous one's pedagogy and no matter how well planned one's response, the adult cannot predict the child's question, nor the meanings that child will make from the knowledge one offers in response" (p. 543). This is another blow to the myth of teacher control. Even so, I feel my anxiety rise when I consider the potential and uncontrollable effects of my curricula on the young people in my classroom. I feel the urge to exert control through shutting down the topic itself in an effort to protect or shelter those in my charge—as though not talking about something makes it go away; as though avoiding race isn't the threat itself.

We cannot avoid race, but neither can we address it tidily within an ordered worldview. The complexity, messiness, and immorality of racism resist such an address. Farley calls on a new kind of sense-making of historical injustice. She identifies and critiques our desire to make sense of historical wrongs pedagogically by imbuing them with meaning in familiar contexts, so we might learn from them. She cites Lévinas, who "finds hope in the opposite trajectory, that is, in the impossibility of making from past trauma a moral lesson; what is hopeful, for Lévinas, is to preserve the 'uselessness of suffering'" (Farley, 2009, p. 547). This challenges a foundational belief of my social justice curricula, which have been predicated precisely on making a moral lesson from past trauma. I can scarcely imagine a unit that does *not* do this, especially when I consider how making use of Others' suffering has been central to the empathetic relationship I've sought to cultivate in my privileged students.

Rather, Farley proposes a pedagogy that challenges the certainty many teachers consider the basis for instruction. How are we supposed to teach what we aren't sure of? Much of my own prep work involves making sure that I feel an intellectual command of the material I am to teach. For Farley, when certainty and resolution are requisites for instruction, teachers are left without effective pedagogical access to complicated and important subjects like racial oppression. In other words, insofar as our objective has been to make pedagogical sense of historical racism, we have struggled.

I'm reminded of the hesitation I've encountered (and afforded!) when I or anyone asks, "What should I do?" when confronted with complicity in racism and White supremacy. I now wonder if that hesitation represented a reading into the question; what uncertainty within myself did I hope to alleviate by being told what to do? The tension of uncertainty and not knowing might be the most generative space in education, and as a teacher I've felt myself loathe to surrender it. Farley assures me that my role as a pedagogue is indeed to lean into the hope that arises when we give ourselves and our students permission to be not only disillusioned but re-illusioned. By confronting our difficult histories and knowledges deliberately, courageously, and with care, we can move those spaces of uncertainty from the margins to the centers of our pedagogy. This new approach is desperately needed:

> Boler argues that empathy does not necessarily lead to awareness of how to engage in action to bring change. Therefore, a critical exposure to discomfort or suffering and pain—that is, one which promotes not only knowledge but also action for change—is needed. (Zembylas, 2015, p. 172)

My pedagogy has taken up empathy and lacked this action orientation, but I can no longer deny it; the suffering of Others cannot edify without cruelty. An ethical treatment of difficult knowledges and histories must neither avoid them nor force them into tidy pedagogical or narrative frames. Rather, we can permit a generative and necessarily risky space within which we and our students can wrestle with ourselves and our difficult historical context.

Rather than making sure I have my facts straight, what if my teaching preparation work focused on an embodied commitment to staying with the discomfort of uncertainty and unknowability, spaces that might well offer meaningful antiracist potential? We know that we cannot make use of suffering within tidy lesson plans and units. Because we cannot both do antiracist classroom work and studiously avoid big feelings, our pedagogy benefits from embracing the "uncertainty, disruption and conflict" inherent to learning (p. 547). We benefit from permitting an uncertainty, even a measure of despair, in our classroom conversations, so that we can permit the space for what Farley (2009) calls "re-illusionment." As a classroom teacher this feels risky to me, and I can imagine that to a classroom teacher invested in a disciplined classroom environment, it might sound downright dangerous. My embodied commitment to uncertainty and unknowability reminds me of the profound failures of conventional schooling to address systemic racism, and that whatever control of knowledge and learning I believe in is illusory. As Farley (2009) says, "We are in the realm of hope—and not mere wishing—when we make meaning in relation to a world without the illusions we use to protect ourselves from what is difficult" (p. 546). To locate our pedagogy in uncertainty and the threat of despair is a radical hope. I believe we benefit from embracing this hope.

As explored here, schooling as most of us know it is hindering rather than helping this pedagogy. Antiracism will depend on moving beyond traditional modes of education in ways we might struggle to imagine, much less enact. Remember, our role as teachers is not to tell students what to do (as if we know!), but to unencumber them of the detrimental blocks with which White people and our ancestors have burdened them. In this work, they are our best and closest allies, and we can be theirs.

FUTURE WORK

There are several potential avenues of future study. First, while planning this work, I had little sense of the role of emotion or embodiment on White students' race talk. Additionally, while I understood White privilege models of racism to be unproductive, I did not anticipate the depressive effect it would have on White students' capacity to imagine antiracism, or that those who resisted it would seem more able to examine Whiteness. Spending more time unpacking the felt experiences of White people as they encounter or participate in race talk could provide valuable insight. In particular, I am excited about the scholarship of shame, as explored in the last few chapters. Relatedly, I believe that interoception, the sense-making process of our bodies, is the most powerful tool in our fight against White supremacy, and our work will benefit from better understanding and practicing that process.

Second, I remain curious about the ways gender and class intersect with Whiteness. My participants shared their thoughts and experiences as members of a social group, which shaped their understandings and discourses. I wonder how gender and class operate within Whiteness to shape individual attitudes about race that might diverge from those represented here. While threads of thought on gender and Whiteness were taken up here, I believe they could provide additional insight on antiracist work. I am eager to delve more deeply into these interconnected topics.

Finally, this work ought to dedicate time and energy to better understanding young White people who think of themselves as conservative and have resisted WPP. Not only can we better understand the counterproductive work being done by WPP, by making sense of their resistance we can work to redirect that resistance toward White supremacy, likely its more appropriate target.

I propose the following questions as guides to future work: What is the relationship between WPP, gender, and being a "good" student? In what ways can the resistance to WPP be repurposed by antiracist educators? In what ways can embodiment and emotional competence work benefit antiracist work? Can addressing and reconfiguring our understandings of shame benefit the antiracist possibilities of young White people? How might any of these projects operate within our education system? And finally, what will it look like to guide other White teachers beyond WPP?

I believe these questions are best answered through in-depth interviews and critical discourse analysis, so researchers can allow participants to excavate deeply held notions of the self and the world in nuanced ways. Because of the workings of Whiteness explored in Chapter 2, accessing these beliefs will take the time and trust of all involved. My confidence in young people to undertake this work is all the more resolute now. I believe they are best positioned to guide the rest of us in recognizing, deconstructing, and working against White supremacy.

CONCLUSION

Our pedagogical work must address Whiteness and White supremacy rather than supposed deficiencies in BIPoC, focus antiracist work on structural racisms rather than individual racisms, and prioritize action and participation rather than conversation and reflection. To conclude, I return to my conversations with Ben. First, I hope we can benefit from the hindsight Ben shared on the perceived failure of his presentation on racism and shame: "I don't think I really communicated that the awkwardness that some people felt was just as notable as whether we were all like super bright [and] productive." I am reminded of the epigraph to this book from Sara Ahmed and find this insight particularly helpful for this work. Antiracism seeks to operate beyond our current ways of thinking. Our work does not abide pedagogical units or rubrics, and it cannot be evaluated in those terms. I opened this book with Sara Ahmed's suggestion that our work find new rubrics for success, that even moments of perceived failure can be productive. Awkward silences and poorly articulated fears can be steps in the right direction, so long as we remain clear-headed about our goals.

Second, near the end of an afternoon conversation, I asked Ben how he managed to be so open about his own thinking on race when his peers so clearly struggled to do so:

> At first I got a few positive responses to just being honest. And then that sort of triggered me to just be honest as a defense mechanism. Like I would be honest, just bluntly honest, in the hopes that my honesty alone would make me worthy of some sort of acceptance.

I had thought Ben was somehow emotionally at peace with race, or possessed astonishing courage in his willingness to be vulnerable, but as he explained to me, he wasn't enlightened or defenseless. I am reminded that we are all in this work together, and that while some of us have studied race academically, we all wrestle with it. Additionally, my antiracism as a White person cannot be dependent on the approval of some governing body of racial authority, including people of color. As hooks wrote, "Anti-racist white folks recognize that their ongoing resistance to White supremacism is genuine when it is not determined in any way by the approval or disapproval of people of color" (as quoted in Tanner, 2014, p. 196).

At the same time, like many of the participants, Ben demonstrated an impressive embrace of vulnerability and uncertainty, qualities that should guide our antiracist work. I asked Ben what was on his mind at the end of one of our conversations, which I propose as our final reflection:

Ben: So right now I feel like I've kinda . . . you know how like in movies when they, like you see, or on TV shows when you see like pigs hanging up in like a slaughterhouse, like in a freezer, they slice open the bellies and the guts come out?

Kevin: You feel like all of your guts are out?

Ben: Well, not just guts, but thoughts.

Kevin: Yeah. And it's kind of a, a mess?

Ben: Yeah, it's kind of a mess. But I kinda like it. I've been kind of telling myself to like that feeling just because I know it's good.

Kevin: Uh, I mean, I imagine it's, vulnerable. Yeah?

Ben: Yeah.

Kevin: I mean I wouldn't want to be, I wouldn't want to be one of those pigs. [laughing] I guess, in that metaphor.

Ben: Yeah, I guess not. What's getting eaten, then, in this metaphor?

Kevin: What's getting eaten?

Ben: Yeah. What is being eaten?

Kevin: I guess—whatever, I mean if we follow the pig thing, whatever's left after all the thoughts come out. I don't know how true that is.

Ben: Huh. Yeah, that feels right.

Here Ben recognizes the significance of what I miss: important aspects of race work lie beyond our thinking selves, beyond our language and reason. Menakem (2017) agrees:

For the past three decades, we've earnestly tried to address white-body supremacy in America with reason, principles, and ideas—using dialogue, forums, discussions, education, and mental training. But the widespread destruction of Black bodies continues. . . . It's not that we've been lazy or insincere. But we've focused our efforts in the wrong direction. We've tried to teach our brains to think better about race. But white-body supremacy doesn't live in our thinking brains. It lives and breathes in our bodies. (pp. 4–5)

Our antiracist work must follow it there.

Ultimately, by developing our and young people's capacity to both understand and be mindful of emotions, we as teachers can foster classrooms better suited to the challenging work of race talk. There is no single guidance for addressing race with anyone, including young White people. Because race and race talk are so contextual and experiential, there are likely as many successful strategies as there are young White people. Moreover, strategies shift with our understanding of ourselves as raced people, so that antiracist strategies from 20 years ago, such as WPP, are now rightfully criticized and built on. That said, the stories in this project can offer approaches that could be more helpful. We cannot hope (nor should we) to develop a static platform from which we can enact antiracism in "teacher-proof" ways. Yet we can empower teachers to foster healthy environments suited to difficult conversation in order to address them more deftly in their own contexts. I hope I have provided some frameworks from which this work can more productively be undertaken.

I write this during an era-defining worldwide pandemic. Once again, our society is wracked with divisions along the typical lines. In addition to the solidarity of shared experiences, however individually experienced, there is apprehension, misdirection, and all-too-familiar patterns of racist scapegoating and disproportionate harm to communities of color. White people seem both less affected by and less resilient to the social and economic effects of the virus. Moreover, in the way any crisis enables clarity, it is possible to witness the failures of our economic and social structures in real time; that a "return to normal" is neither possible nor desirable. Perhaps part of what we, especially White people, can take away from this is a heightened awareness of ourselves and the not-so-hidden ways we are all interconnected.

Endnotes

Chapter 1

1. While "Black" is now capitalized for most style manuals, whether to capitalize "White" remains a debate. (Teachers College [TC] Press style manual calls for any specific racial group to be capitalize [e.g., "Black," "Hispanic,"] but not "people of color." This is also debated, and I expect the phrase "people of color" will be capitalized or abandoned in the coming years.) In this work, I follow the style manual of TC Press in an effort to recognize Whiteness as representing a specific set of values, norms, and customs, however damaging and problematic.

2. Neoliberalism is shorthand for a free-market, highly individualized worldview typical of conservative politics and economics in the late 20th century. For more, see Zachary Casey's (2016) *A Pedagogy of Anticapitalist Antiracism: Whiteness, Neoliberalism, and Resistance in Education*.

3. The acronym BIPoC refers to Black, Indigenous, and people of color. Even as of this writing, when the term is relatively new, the acronym is criticized in several ways. In all likelihood, the language will have changed by the time the book is in circulation.

Chapter 2

1. In an effort to highlight the process of racialization, I capitalize "Others" when the term is used to designate a group of people raced by White supremacy.

2. Importantly, Bacon's rebellion began as a crusade against neighboring Indigenous groups before turning on colonial leadership.

3. For a thorough, heartbreaking take on how economic interest drove slavery, as well as how slavery shaped contemporary economics, see Edward Baptist's (2014) text *The Half Has Never Been Told*.

4. For more on the minstrel lineage of hip-hop, see W. T. Lhamon's (1998) *Raising Cain*.

5. I've also wondered about the legitimating racial role played by the Black back-up bands and bandleaders to White late-night TV hosts, including Kevin Eubanks to Jay Leno, The Roots to Jimmy Fallon, and Jon Batiste to Stephen Colbert.

6. Among the many histories passed over in this abbreviated telling, post-bellum Southern reconstruction, with its racial progress and violent White backlash, is perhaps the most conspicuous. For more, see "The General Strike" (chapter 4) in *Black Reconstruction in America: 1860–1880* by W. E. B. Du Bois (1992).

7. Of course, the condemned, stereotypical, anti-industrial behavior of the Irish also persisted in the term "Paddy Wagon," derogatory slang for a police van called on to arrest drunken Irish. For more, see Noel Ignatiev's (1995) *How the Irish Became White.*

8. While the Constitution clearly lays out the three-fifths clause, along with many other racist laws concerning slavery, the words *slave* and *slavery* are never used (Kendi, 2016).

9. For more, see Matthew Frye Jacobson's (1998) *Whiteness of a Different Color: European Immigrants and the Alchemy of Race.*

10. Color celebrate (DiAngelo, 2018), where White people claim an affinity for "diversity" or Black friends, serves a similar function.

11. While similar in ways, Mica Pollock's (2004) colormuteness focuses more on patterns of silence and avoidance around race at a more structural level, while White silence tends to refer to the silence performed by White individuals.

Chapter 3

1. As will become clear, working away from the alignment of "liberal" with antiracism and "conservative" with racial prejudice is central to reimagining White antiracism, both because of the inaccuracy of that view and the deeply unhelpful impact on both liberal- and conservative-affiliated White people.

2. For a more in-depth examination of Whiteness and film, see Richard Dyer's (1997) *White* or Matthew Hughey's (2014) *The White Savior Film: Content, Critics, and Consumption.*

3. Spectrum is the name of a senior-level interdisciplinary social justice–oriented course at St Ann's.

4. The tense celebration of ideological "balance" in education (or in other sources of information) has a long history, explored in part by Rick Lybeck (2015).

5. Note how David uses *African American* rather than *Black*, an example of Heidi's suggestion that in moments of uncertainty she might revert to *African American*, what David later noted is used by White people trying to sound more "woke."

6. While several participants struggled with language around race, Ken in particular used unfamiliar syntax when talking about race worthy of its own study; for another example: "John, he was pretty diverse at school. He had friends in the white, and black. He didn't really think about that stuff." This felt like an example, if more dramatic, of the participants' struggle with language around race.

7. I use *perform* here as Sara Ahmed (2004b) does in her critique "Declarations of Whiteness: The Non-Performativity of Anti-Racism," where the "performance" of antiracism through proclamations serves to reinscribe racist structures and norms.

Chapter 4

1. I want to note the enormous potential for antiracist work within the arts, in particular theater. I've heard from several students that the only two teachers at St Ann's who talk about race are the theater teacher and myself. See also Augusto Boal's (1993) *Theater of the Oppressed*.

2. #MeToo was introduced as a social movement over a decade earlier by activist and sexual assault survivor Tarana Burke, a Black woman. This history has been eclipsed by primarily White actors.

3. As noted earlier, Ken often used what felt to me like "the-quiet-part-out-loud" language in his race talk, though if he was aware that his speech was awkward, he never let on.

4. For example, see *White Trash* (Isenberg, 2017).

5. Augusto Boal (1995), creator of *Theater of the Oppressed*, challenged the function of theater for change as a catharsis that left an audience with a sense of closure. He called for an anti-catharsis whereby an audience would resolve only what stood in their way, retaining all the tension and energy of an unresolved problem so that they might work to resolve the problem in the world. As he said, "a catharsis of detrimental blocks!" (p. 73).

Chapter 5

1. Importantly, this is not the racial apathy Forman and Lewis (2006) described as "not caring and not knowing" (p. 175).

2. Mica Pollock's (2004) *Colormute* identified a set of paradoxical aspects of race talk in similar terms. For example, *"We don't belong to simple racial groups, but we do"* and *"Race doesn't matter, but it does"* (pp. 13–14, emphasis in original).

3. Importantly, double-binds are commonly experienced by marginalized groups (e.g., BIPoC folks and women might be encouraged to share their experiences in "safe spaces," only to be dismissed, tone policed, or be denied entirely).

4. Levine-Rasky (2000) makes this case as well.

5. For more on affect, see Ahmed (2004a), Zembylas (2006), and Leonardo and Zembylas (2013).

Chapter 6

1. For more on melancholia, see Anne Anlin Cheng's (2001) brilliant *The Melancholy of Race*.

2. Racial affinity groups provide a forum wherein White people can process their Whiteness without burdening or risking injury to people of color.

Such groups can also afford people of color a space to share experiences and frustrations without the risk of those experiences being dismissed by White people. While the teacher trainings I conduct are not exclusive to White educators, they are voluntary and designed to provide White teachers space to process and become accountable for their Whiteness among other White people. Other such White affinity organizations include SURJ, Showing Up for Racial Justice (surj.org).

3. Leonardo and Porter (2010) explore how "safe" spaces in classrooms, by failing to question "for whose safety," typically serve to protect White students from experiencing productive racial discomfort as well as to silence the experiences of students of color.

4. For more, see Matthew Hughey's (2014) *The White Savior Film.*

5. This "anticatharsis" recalls Boal's (1993) work in *Theatre of the Oppressed,* where "spect-actors" work to identify and eliminate the obstacles inhibiting action by the bystander/oppressed. For more, see Boal's (1995) *Rainbow of Desire.*

6. The scholarship of witnessing is profoundly influenced by Dori Laub and Shoshana Felman, who developed the theory as part of their work of passing on the stories of the holocaust of WWII.

Chapter 7

1. As Chanequa Walker-Barnes (2017) wrote, "We must align with one another in ways that embody the society that we are attempting to build." For more, see *emergent strategy* by adrienne marie brown (2017).

2. By its nature, precarity is a place of deep potential. For more on the affordances of precarity, see Zembylas (2019).

3. This phenomenon is called *the backfire effect,* or *confirmation bias,* well examined here: https://theoatmeal.com/comics/believe.

References

Ahmad, A. (2015). *A note on call-out culture*. Briarpatch. https://briarpatchmagazine
.com/articles/view/a-note-on-call-out-culture

Ahmed, S. (2004a). *The cultural politics of emotion*. University of Edinburgh Press.

Ahmed, S. (2004b). Declarations of Whiteness: The non-performativity of anti-racism. *Borderlands, 3*(2), https://research.gold.ac.uk/id/eprint/13911

Ahmed, S. (2007). A phenomenology of Whiteness. *Feminist Theory, 8*(2), 149–168.

Alexander, M. (2012). *The new Jim Crow: Mass incarceration in the Age of colorblindness*. The New Press.

Allen, T. (2012). *The invention of the White race, vol 2: The origin of racial oppression in Anglo-America*. Verso.

Ambrosio, J. (2014). Teaching the psychosocial subject: White students and racial privilege. *International Journal of Qualitative Studies in Education, 27*(10), 1376–1394.

Applebaum, B. (2016). "Listening silence" and its discursive effects. *Educational Theory, 66*(3), 389–404.

Banks, A. (2016). Are group cues necessary? How anger makes ethnocentrism among Whites a stronger predictor of racial and immigration policy opinions. *Political Behavior, 38*(3), 635–657.

Baptist, E. E. (2014). *The half has never been told: Slavery and the making of American capitalism*. Basic Books.

Biewen, J. (Producer). (2018, January 29). *Scene on radio: Seeing White* [audio podcast]. sceneonradio.org/seeing-white/

Boal, A. (1993). *Theatre of the oppressed*. Theater Communications Group.

Boal, A. (1995). *Rainbow of Desire*. Routledge.

Boler, M. (1999). *Feeling power: Emotions and education*. Routledge.

Bonilla-Silva, E. (2014). *Racism without racists: Color-blind racism and the persistence of racial inequality in the United States*. Rowman and Littlefield.

Bonilla-Silva, E., & Forman, T. (2000). "I am not a racist, but . . .": Mapping White college students' racial ideology in the USA. *Discourse & Society, 11*(1), 50–85.

Borsheim-Black, C., & Sarigianedes, S. (2019). *Letting go of literary Whiteness: Antiracist literary instruction for white students*. Teachers College Press.

Britzman, D. (1991). *Practice makes practice: A critical study of learning to teach.* SUNY Press.

Britzman, D. P. (2000). If the story cannot end: Deferred action, ambivalence, and difficult knowledge. In R. I. Simon, S. Rosenberg, & C. Eppert (Eds.), *Between hope and despair: The pedagogical encounter of historical remembrance* (pp. 27–57). Rowman & Littlefield.

brown, a. m. (2017). *emergent strategy: shaping change, changing worlds.* AK Press.

Bucholtz, M. (2011). *White kids: Language, race, and styles of youth identity.* Cambridge University Press.

Casey, Z. (2016) *A pedagogy of anticapitalist antiracism: Whiteness, neoliberalism, and resistance in education.* SUNY Press.

Cheng, A. A. (2001). *The melancholy of race: Psychoanalysis, assimilation, and hidden grief.* Oxford University Press.

Chinoyowa, C. (2013). A matter of "knowledge in the blood"? Unperforming racial and ethnic prejudice in tertiary educational spaces in South Africa. *African Conflict and Peacebuilding Review, 3*(2), 91–109.

Chubbuck, S. M., & Zembylas, M. (2008). The emotional ambivalence of socially just teaching: A case study of a novice urban schoolteacher. *American Educational Research Journal, 45*(2), 274–318.

Coates, T. (2015). *Between the world and me.* Random House.

Deloria, P. (1998). *Playing Indian.* Yale University Press.

DiAngelo, R. (2018). *White fragility: Why it's so hard for White people to talk about racism.* Beacon.

Du Bois, W. E. B. (1992). *Black reconstruction in America.* The Free Press. Original work published in 1903

Du Bois, W. E. B. (1995). *The souls of Black folk.* Signet Classic. Original work published in 1935

DuVernay, A. (2015). *Selma* [Motion picture]. United States, Paramount Pictures.

Dyer, R. (1997). *White.* Routledge.

Ellison, R. (1995). *Shadow and act.* Vintage. (Original work published in 1953)

Farley, L. (2009). Radical hope: Or, the problem of uncertainty in history education. *Curriculum Inquiry, 39*(4), 537–554.

Fine, M. (1994). Dis-stance and other stances: Negotiations of power inside feminist research. In A. Gitlin (Ed.), *Power and method: Political activism and educational research* (pp. 13–35). Routledge.

Forman, T. A., & Lewis, A. E. (2006). Racial apathy and hurricane Katrina: The social anatomy of prejudice in the post-Civil Rights era. *Du Bois Review 3*(1), 175–202.

Frankenberg, R. (1993). *White women, race matters.* University of Minnesota Press.

Freire, P. (2007). *Pedagogy of the oppressed.* Continuum.

Fromm, E. (2000). *The art of loving.* Perennial.

Frost, L. (2005). *Never one nation: Freaks, savages, and whiteness in U.S. popular culture, 1850–1877*. University of Minnesota Press.

Gallagher, C. (1997). Redefining racial privilege in the United States. *Transformations, 8*(1), 1–28.

Gardner, R. (2017). Discussing racial trauma using visual thinking strategies. *Language Arts, 94*(5), 338–345.

Gay, G., & Kirkland, K. (2003). Developing cultural critical consciousness and self-reflection in preservice teacher education. *Theory into Practice, 42*, 181–187.

Gibneyt, P. (2006). The double bind theory: Still crazy-making after all these years. *Psychotherapy in Australia, 12*(3), 48–55.

Gigliotti, D. (Producer), & Melfi, T. (Director). (2016). *Hidden figures* [Motion picture]. United States, 20th Century Fox.

Guinier, L. (2004). From racial liberalism to racial literacy: *Brown v. Board of Education* and the interest-divergence dilemma. *The Journal of American History, 19*(1), 92–118.

Hamel, T. M. (2019). *The body talks back: An embodied expansion of critical consciousness* (Publication No. 22585187) [Doctoral dissertation].

Haney López, I. A. (2013). *Dog whistle politics: How coded racial appeals have reinvented racism and wrecked the middle class*. Oxford University Press.

Hochschild, A. (2016). *Strangers in their own land*. The New Press.

Hughey, M. (2014). *The White savior film: Content, critics, and consumption*. Temple University Press.

Ignatiev, N. (1995). *How the Irish became white*. Routledge.

Isenberg, N. (2017). *White trash: A 400-year untold history of class in America*. Penguin.

Jacobson, M. (1998). *Whiteness of a different color: European immigrants and the alchemy of race*. Harvard University Press.

Jansen, J. (2009). *Knowledge in the blood: Confronting race and the apartheid past*. Stanford University Press.

Joffe-Walt, C. (Host) (2020). *Nice White parents* [audio podcast]. Serial Productions and *The New York Times*. https://www.nytimes.com/2020/07/23/podcasts/nice-white-parents-serial.html

Jupp, J. C., & Slattery, G. P. (2010). Becoming teachers of inner-city students: Identification creativity and curriculum wisdom of committed White male teachers. *Urban Education, 47*(1), 280–311.

Kendi, I. X. (2016). *Stamped from the beginning: The definitive history of racist ideas in America*. Nation Books.

Kenney, L. D. (2000). Doing my homework: The autoethnography of a White teenage girl. In F. W. Twine & J. Warren (Eds.), *Racing research, researching race: Methodological dilemmas in critical race studies* (pp. 111–133). NYU Press.

Kincheloe, J. L., & McLaren, P. (2005). Rethinking critical theory and qualitative research. In N. K. Denzin & Y. S. Lincoln (Eds.), *The handbook of qualitative research* (3rd ed., pp. 303–342). SAGE.

King, M. L., Jr. (2018). *Letter from Birmingham jail*. Penguin Classics. (Original work published in 1963)

King, R. (2018). *Mindful of race: Transforming racism from the inside out*. Sounds True.

Kumashiro, K. (2002) *Troubling education: Queer activism and antioppressive pedagogy*. Routledge.

Ladson-Billings, G., & Tate, W. F. (1995). Toward a critical race theory of education. *Teachers College Record, 97*, 47–68.

Lee-Nichols, M., & Tierney, J. D. (2018). The colorblind conundrum: Seeing and not seeing color in White rural schools. In S. McManimon, Z. Casey, & C. Berchini (Eds.), *Whiteness at the table: Antiracism, racism, and identity in education* (pp. 49–63). Lexington.

Lensmire, T., McManimon, S., Tierney, J. D., Lee-Nichols, M., Casey, Z., Lensmire, A., & Davis, B. (2013). McIntosh as synecdoche: Education's focus on White privilege undermines antiracism. *Harvard Educational Review, 83*(3), 410–432.

Lensmire, T. J. (2010). Ambivalent White racial identities: Fear and an elusive innocence. *Race Ethnicity and Education, 13*(2), 159–172.

Lensmire, T. J. (2017). White anti-racists and belonging. *Whiteness and Education, 2*(1), 4–14.

Lensmire, T. J. (2018). Introduction. In S. K. McManimon, Z. A. Casey, & C. Berchini (Eds.), *Whiteness at the table* (pp. 1–4). Lexington.

Leonardo, Z. (2004). The color of supremacy: Beyond the discourse of "white privilege." *Educational Philosophy & Theory, 36*(2), 137–152.

Leonardo, Z., & Porter, R. K. (2010). Pedagogy of fear: Toward a Fanonian theory of "safety" in race dialogue. *Race, Ethnicity and Education, 13*(2), 139–157.

Leonardo, Z., & Zembylas, M. (2013). Whiteness as technology of affect: Implications for educational praxis. *Equity & Excellence in Education, 46*(1), 150–165.

Levine-Rasky, C. (2000). Framing Whiteness: Working through the tensions in introducing Whiteness to educators. *Race Ethnicity and Education, 3*(3), 271–292.

Lewis, A., & Diamond, J. (2015). *Despite the best intentions: How racial inequality thrives in good schools*. Oxford University Press.

Lhamon, W. T. (1998). *Raising Cain: Blackface performance from Jim Crow to hip hop*. Harvard University Press.

Linder, C. (2015). Navigating guilt, shame, and fear of appearing racist: A conceptual model of antiracist White feminist identity development. *Journal of College Student Development, 56*(6), 535–550.

Lindquist, J. (2004). Class affects, classroom affectations: Working through the paradoxes of strategic empathy. *Social Class and English Studies, 67*(2), 187–209.

Logue, J. (2005). Deconstructing privilege: A contrapuntal approach. *Philosophy of Education*, 371–379.

Lott, E. (1995). *Love and theft: Blackface minstrelsy and the American working class*. Oxford University Press.

Lucas, J. (2017, November 28). *Joyner Lucas—I'm not racist* [Video]. https://www.youtube.com/watch?v=43gm3CJePn0

Lybeck, R. (2015). *Fear and reconciliation: The U.S.-Dakota way in White public pedagogy* [Unpublished doctoral dissertation]. University of Minnesota.

Manne, K. (2018). Melancholy Whiteness (or, shame-faced in shadows). *Philosophy and Phenomenological Research*, *96*(1), 233–242.

Margolin, L. (2015). Unpacking the invisible knapsack: The invention of White privilege pedagogy. *Cogent Social Sciences*, *1*(1). http://dx.doi.org/10.1080/23311886.2015.1053183

Matias, C. (2012). Who you callin' White?! A critical counter-story on colouring White identity. *Race Ethnicity and Education*, *16*(3), 291–315.

Matias, C. (2016). *Feeling White: Whiteness, emotionality, and education (cultural pluralism, democracy, socio-environmental justice and education)*. Sense.

May, V. (2015). *Pursuing intersectionality, unsettling dominant imaginaries*. Routledge.

McGhee, H. (2021). *The sum of us: What racism costs us all and how we can prosper together*. One World Press.

McIntosh, P. (1988). *White privilege and male privilege: A personal account of coming to see correspondences through work in women's studies* [Working paper 189]. Wellesley Center for Research on Women.

Melamed, J. (2011). *Represent and destroy: Rationalizing violence in the new racial capitalism*. University of Minnesota Press.

Memmi, A. (1965). *The colonized and the colonizer*. Boston, MA: Beacon Press.

Menakem, R. (2017). *My grandmother's hands: Racialized trauma and the pathway to mending our hearts and bodies*. Central Recovery Press.

Mills, C. W. (1997). *The racial contract*. Cornell University Press.

Mitchell, T. (2008). Traditional vs. critical service-learning: Engaging the literature to differentiate two models. *Michigan Journal of Community Service Learning*, 50–65.

Morrison, T. (1992). *Playing in the dark: Whiteness and the literary imagination*. Harvard University Press.

Mun Wah, L. (Producer, Director). (1994). *The color of fear* [Motion picture]. Berkeley, CA: Stir-Fry Productions.

Ozawa v. United States, 206 U.S. 178 (1922)

Peck, R. (Director). (2016). *I am not your Negro* [Motion picture]. United States, Magnolia Pictures.

Perry, P. (2002). *Shades of white: White kids and racial identities in high school*. Duke University Press.

Pollock, M. (2004). *Colormute: Race talk dilemmas in an American school*. Princeton University Press.

Pratt, M. B. (1984). Identity: Skin, blood, heart. In E. Bulkin, M. B. Pratt, & B. Smith (Eds.), *Yours in struggle: Three feminist perspectives on anti-Semitism and racism* (pp. 1–57). Firebrand Books.

Roberts, R., Bell, L., & Murphy, B. (2008). Flipping the script: Analyzing youth talk about race and racism. *Anthropology & Education Quarterly, 39*(3), 334–354.

Roediger, D. (1991). *The wages of Whiteness.* Verso.

Rollins v. State, 92 So. 35 (Ala. Ct App. 1922)

Ross, L. (2019, August 17). I'm a Black feminist. I think call-out culture is toxic. *The New York Times.* https://www.nytimes.com/2019/08/17/opinion/sunday/cancel-culture-call-out.html

Schaefer, D. (2019). Whiteness and civilization: Shame, race, and the rhetoric of Donald Trump. *Communication and Critical/Cultural Studies, 17*(1), 1–18. https://doi.org/10.1080/14791420.2019.1667503

Shabazz, R. (n.d.). *12 major corporations benefiting from the prison industrial complex.* http://maltajusticeinitiative.org/12-major-corporations-benefiting-from-the-prison-industrial-complex-2/

Sher, S. (Producer), & Tarantino, Q. (Director). 2012. *Django unchained* [Motion picture]. United States, The Weinstein Company.

Snyder-Young, D. (2010). Beyond "an aesthetic of objectivity": Performance ethnography, performance texts, and theatricality. *Qualitative Inquiry, 16*(10), 883–893.

Stone, M. (1976). *When God was a woman.* Mariner Books.

Stowe, H. B. (1852) *Uncle Tom's Cabin.* J. Cassell.

Tanner, S. J. (2018). Whiteness is a White problem: Whiteness in English education. *English Education, 51*(2), 182–199.

Taylor, T. (Producer & Director). (2011). *The Help* [Motion picture]. United States, Walt Disney Studios.

Thandeka. (2001). *Learning to be White: Money, race, and God in America.* Continuum.

Thomas, E. (2015). "We always talk about race": Navigating race talk dilemmas in the teaching of literature. *Research in the Teaching of English, 50*(2), 154–175.

Trainor, J. S. (2002). Critical pedagogy's "other": Constructions of Whiteness in education for social change. *College Composition and Communication, 53*(4), 631–650.

Trainor, J. S. (2008). *Rethinking racism: Emotion, persuasion and literacy education in an all-White high school.* Southern Illinois University Press.

United States v. Bhagat Singh Thind, 261 U.S. 204 (1923)

U.S. Department of Justice, Civil Rights Division. (2015, March 4). *Investigation on the Ferguson Police Department.* https://www.justice.gov/sites/default/files/opa/press-releases/attachments/2015/03/04/ferguson_police_department_report.pdf

Utt, J. (2015, May 25) *Hey White people! If you really want to help end racism, you need to invest in other White people (Yeah, we know it sounds counterintuitive)*. Everyday Feminism. https://everydayfeminism.com/2015/05/invest-in-other-white-people/

van der Kolk, B. (2015). *The body keeps the score: Brain, mind, and body in the healing of trauma*. Penguin.

Vaught, S. (2017). *Compulsory: Education and the dispossession of youth in a prison school*. University of Minnesota Press.

Vemuri, A. (2018). "Calling out" campus sexual violence: Student activist labors of confrontation and fear. *Communication Culture & Critique, 11*, 498–502.

Winans, A. (2010). Cultivating racial literacy in White, segregated settings: Emotions as site of ethical engagement and inquiry. *Curriculum Inquiry, 40*(3), 475–491.

Wright, R. (2005). *Native son*. Perennial Classics.

Zembylas, M. (2006). Witnessing in the classroom: The ethics and politics of affect. *Educational Theory, 56*(34), 305–324.

Zembylas, M. (2012). Pedagogies of strategic empathy: Navigating through the emotional complexities of antiracism in higher education. *Teaching in Higher Education, 17*(2), 113–125.

Zembylas, M. (2013). Critical pedagogy and emotion: Working through "troubled knowledge" in posttraumatic contexts. *Critical Studies in Education, 54*(2), 176–189.

Zembylas, M. (2014). Theorizing "difficult knowledge" in the aftermath of the "affective turn": Implications for curriculum and pedagogy in handling traumatic representations. *Curriculum Inquiry, 44*(3), 390–412.

Zembylas, M. (2015). "Pedagogy of discomfort" and its ethical implications: The tensions of ethical violence in social justice education. *Ethics and Education, 10*(2), 163–174.

Zembylas, M. (2019). "Shame at being human" as a transformative concept and praxis: Pedagogical possibilities. *Feminism and Psychology, 29*(2), 303–321.

Zembylas, M. (2020). The affective modes of right-wing populism: Trump pedagogy and lessons for democratic education. *Studies in Philosophy and Education, 39*, 151–166.

Index

Note: Page numbers followed by n and number represent endnotes and note number respectively.

About the Author

Kevin Lally is a Whiteness scholar who has taught English in the Twin Cities for 2 decades. His work explores the harmful mechanisms of Whiteness, including White privilege pedagogy, and looks beyond the stuckness of White shame and guilt to new, more generative models of antiracism for White people in education. He has presented his work on Whiteness nationally and conducts workshops on Whiteness in education for teachers through the Minnesota Writing Project. Kevin earned his PhD in curriculum and instruction from the University of Minnesota in 2020. In addition to teaching high school English Language Arts, Kevin teaches education courses in the Twin Cities area.